TV Talk
Show Hosts

TV TALK SHOW HOSTS

This publication is not sponsored or endorsed by, or otherwise affiliated with, any of the celebrities, shows or networks mentioned within. Any opinions expressed are solely those of the authors.

Photo Credits: clockwise from right: front cover – AP/WWP (Rosie O'Donnell), Christopher Little/CBS/Liaison (David Letterman), Everett Collection (Sally Jesse Raphael), AP/WWP (Oprah Winfrey), Mitchell Gerber/CORBIS (Jerry Springer)
back cover – Jeff Kravitz/Image Direct (Jay Leno)

EDITORIAL

Managing Editor:	Jeff Mahony
Associate Editors:	Melissa A. Bennett
	Gia C. Manalio
	Mike Micciulla
	Paula Stuckart
Assistant Editors:	Heather N. Carreiro
	Jennifer Renk
	Joan C. Wheal
Editorial Assistants:	Timothy R. Affleck
	Beth Hackett
	Christina M. Sette
	Steven Shinkaruk

WEB

Web Graphic Designer: Ryan Falis

PRODUCTION

Production Manager: Scott Sierakowski

ART

Creative Director:	Joe T. Nguyen
Assistant Art Director:	Lance Doyle
Senior Graphic Designers:	Marla B. Gladstone
	Susannah C. Judd
	David S. Maloney
	Carole Mattia-Slater
	David Ten Eyck
Graphic Designers:	Jennifer J. Bennett
	Sean-Ryan Dudley
	Kimberly Eastman
	Melani Gonzalez
	Jim MacLeod
	Jeremy Maendel
	Chery-Ann Poudrier

R&D

Product Development
Manager: Paul Rasid

ISBN 1-58598-079-X

CheckerBee
PUBLISHING

306 Industrial Park Road
Middletown, CT 06457
www.CheckerBee.com

Table Of Contents

Who Are These People Anyway?™

W ho is that guy in the darkened room who keeps turning up on PBS at night? Or that quirky guy who comes on CBS after David Letterman? They're America's favorite talk show hosts, a fascinating combination of news anchor and television star! Every morning, every afternoon and every night they appear on your television screen to offer up some great commentary, insightful advice and a little light hearted fun.

But what are they like? Have you ever wondered why the unmarried Queen Latifah wears a ring? Or how Sally Jesse Raphael got her start? Maybe you'd like to know where Conan O'Brien went to college, or if Maury Povich has children. If so, this book is where you'll find profiles of all those hosts, and even more!

You'll also get a detailed history of talk shows in America, from the black-and-white days of Dave Garroway up to the modern times of Craig Kilborn. Wonder why Drew Barrymore's birthday interview with David Letterman was talked about so much? Look into the past and relive the talk shows' most memorable moments. Did you wonder if your favorite television personality ever had a show of their own? Reminisce with a history of all those lesser-know shows that never made it.

The Who Are These People Anyway?™ series brings the whole world of celebrities and other interesting people right into your living room. Other books in the series spotlight movie stars, radio show hosts, sports superstars, popular musicians and more! Check out our web site at *www.checkerbee.com* for more details about this series that really sizzles!

TV Talk Shows Throughout Time

Television talk show hosts may be some of the most recognizable figures in today's entertainment world, but their shows are nothing new. In fact, talk shows have been around for as long as there have been televisions to broadcast them. The topics may have changed a bit – but the idea remains the same. Let's take a look at how the combination of information, entertainment and a memorable host has been gracing American television screens for over 50 years. And how these news programs and variety shows through the years have helped to inspire and mold the television talk shows that we all tune in to today.

The 1950s – Coming Into Focus In A Brave New World

While the United States was starting to settle into its post war boom years, many consumers were buying something new called a television set. As the nation began to turn off the radio and tune in to television, many popular radio show hosts knew their days were numbered, and tried to make the move to television. Not all of them made it. But one of the most popular shows that did was *Meet The Press*, which first flickered onto American screens in 1947. Producers Lawrence Spivak and Martha Rountree set about creating a format of news and information that was less like a dry reading and more like a panel discussion. The show remains on the air after over half a century of broadcasting.

With the new popularity of television, NBC created the *Today* show in 1952. Unlike *Meet The Press*, the creators of *Today* were aiming for a more

Dave Garroway and J. Fred Muggs celebrate their five years of *Today* in 1957.

light hearted show, and the easy going charm of Dave Garroway made it a strong success. Of course, it probably didn't hurt things that one of Garroway's co-hosts was a chimpanzee named J. Fred Muggs! Anxious to compete with NBC, the executives at CBS got into the act with the CBS *Morning Show*. Although it didn't last long against the competition, the show was a training ground for such later broadcasting luminaries as Walter Cronkite, Jack Paar and even a young substitute host by the name of Johnny Carson.

At night, sleepy viewers in need of entertainment didn't have too much of a choice. But all of that changed when Steve Allen, a proud veteran of radio, stepped up to the micro-

Steve Allen tickles the ivories with Jayne Meadows and Louis Nye.

phone as host of *Tonight* in 1954. Allen was himself a comic and musician, and never hesitated to include his diverse interests in a show full of music, comedy and plain old charismatic charm.

Allen left the show in 1957, but the new host would go where Allen never had. Jack Paar brought an air of serious news to what had been primarily a variety show. It wasn't any show where you could be entertained by a young Bill Cosby – and hear a personal interview with Robert F. Kennedy!

Talk To The Animals

Today's wild talk shows may sometimes resemble a zoo or a circus, but in the 1950s, talk shows really did belong to the animals! J. Fred Muggs was the first (but not the last) chimp to star on *Today*. Let's hope J. Fred didn't drive the cast bananas!

The 1960s – Heeeeeeeere's Johnny . . . And Mike!

After nearly a decade of waking up American viewers on *Today*, Dave Garroway decided to call it quits in 1961. Baseball legend Joe Garagiola stepped in soon after to add his unique humor to the show. And a young *Today* writer named Barbara Walters was first pressed into service at John F. Kennedy's funeral, creating a new journalistic sensation. But the morning show would soon have company later on in the day.

During the 1960s, a number of celebrities tried to start their own talk shows on daytime television, many of which were geared towards women. Some of these shows focused on the host's own fame and celebrity status, such as Gypsy Rose Lee's show. Others addressed more serious issues, like Helen Gurley Brown's *Outrageous Opinions* in 1967. Merv Griffin actually had two shows on during this time. But none of these shows approached the status of *The Mike Douglas Show*. After going national in 1963, Douglas concentrated on celebrity guests instead of the serious news. The show's popularity led to an Emmy in 1967, the first such award ever given to a talk show.

The Ballad Of John And Yoko (And Mike)

Celebrity guest hosts have long been a tradition of television talk shows, but none have sparked quite as much controversy as John Lennon and Yoko Ono, who took over the *Mike Douglas Show* from February 14-18 in 1972.

After NBC cut one of Jack Paar's jokes in 1960, he fumed off the stage for a while, and finally left *Tonight* in 1962. A succession of guest hosts from Soupy Sales to Groucho Marx filled in for Paar until NBC hired an occasional substitute host named Johnny Carson to work full time. *The Tonight Show Starring Johnny Carson* was an instant hit, due to Carson's prime directive – the show was never supposed to be anything but entertaining! Legions of fans made Carson the undisputed king of late-night television, essentially leaving such competitors as Joey Bishop and Dick Cavett in the dust.

The 1970s – Daytime With Donahue

After playing second fiddle to NBC for the morning time slot, ABC finally got their feet in the door in 1975 with *Good Morning America*. The show's hosts, David Hartman and Nancy Dussault, offered a different spin on the morning news. *Good Morning America* was a show with a relaxed, domestic setting, more like your kitchen table than a news desk. The formula propelled the show above *Today* in the ratings, even though *Today* had come up with a winning combination of hosts in Tom Brokaw, Jane Pauley and Gene Shalit.

In 1967, a young Ohio journalist named Phil Donahue had started his own local television talk show, and stepped into controversy on the first episode by having vocal atheist Madalyn Murray O'Hair as a guest. His show caught momentum, as did his habit of involving his studio audience in anything that happened on stage. By the mid 1970s, *Donahue* was a nationally syndicated daytime show, bringing such topics as birth control and abortion into American living rooms.

From the beginning, Donahue never hesitated to be controversial on his show. By having sex researchers William Masters and Virginia Johnson as guests, Donahue made his show the first to address such matters on television – although it certainly wouldn't be the last!

NBC had found a gold mine in Johnny Carson, as *The Tonight Show* continued to dominate the late-night airwaves. The network tried to follow up Carson's show with *Tomorrow* in 1973, hosted by

Phil Donahue started a whole new trend in television talk shows in the 1970s.

Tom Snyder. Snyder's harsh style was counteracted by the addition of gossip columnist Rona Barrett as his West Coast correspondent.

The 1980s — Oprah And "Tabloid TV"

The addition of Bryant Gumbel to *Today* wasn't enough to get the NBC show back on top. *Good Morning America* still had audiences tuning in to ABC in the morning, especially when Joan Lunden came aboard in 1980, and Charlie Gibson in 1987.

AP/WWP

After Oprah Winfrey graced the screen in 1986, talk shows would never be the same.

In 1983, Phil Donahue found himself with a bit of competition for the afternoon circuit. Radio personality Sally Jessy Raphael burst onto the scene with *The Sally Show*, and gained respect as one of the few female voices on television. Her monopoly didn't last long, however. In 1986, a Baltimore newscaster named Oprah Winfrey moved to Chicago and took her talk show to a national audience. Both Raphael and Winfrey took Donahue's original formula of interviewing everyday people on controversial subjects, but they added their own personality and style to their shows.

But neither of them went as far as their contemporary Geraldo Rivera. When *Geraldo* debuted in 1987, he planned for the format to go ever further, booking guests certain to cause a bit of violence in the studio. Those fears were realized the next year, when a show featuring African-American activist Roy Innis and white supremacists erupted into a brawl that left Rivera with a broken nose.

Although *The Tonight Show* continued to command the most respect on the late-night airwaves, Johnny Carson got a little competition in the 1980s. Tom Snyder was replaced in 1982 by a sarcastic, gap-toothed comic named David Letterman. Shows like *Thicke of the Night* (with Alan Thicke), *The Late Show Starring Joan Rivers* and *The Pat Sajak Show* flared briefly, but none of them lasted more than a year.

Carson's only really serious competition came in 1989, with the premiere of *The Arsenio Hall Show*. Experienced stand-up comic Arsenio Hall turned late-night TV on its ear with guests never before seen on the more standard talk shows, and opened a fresh new youth market up to television.

The 1990s – Afternoons Go Overboard And Johnny Hangs It Up

When Katie Couric joined the cast of *Today* in 1991, she began the audience-pleasing formula which still carries the show today. Bryant Gumbel's 1996 defection to CBS paved the way for Matt Lauer. Al Roker and Ann Curry rounded out the cast, although *Today* still competes with *Good Morning America*.

As *Donahue* entered its last years, a whole new crop of shows and hosts sprang up to fill the near void. Maury Povich and Jenny Jones appeared in 1991, with Leeza Gibbons and Ricki Lake fol-lowing two years later. This new breed of shows was like nothing viewers had ever seen. Phil Donahue had been intellectual, sensitive and serious-minded; the new breed tended to be youth-oriented, silly and willing to push the envelope far beyond anything Donahue had ever done.

The most shocking of all was former Cincinnati mayor Jerry Springer, whose guests never hesitated to act out their differences with enough violence to put professional wrestling to shame!

AP/WWP

"Trash TV" caused concern in many people, including Senator Joseph Lieberman.

Springer's antics prompted an outcry from Connecticut Senator Joseph Lieberman, who called for "trashy TV talk shows to confront junk," and led an all-out boycott of such shows' sponsors. It was not until the 1996 debut of Rosie O'Donnell's popular show that daytime television began to be seen as a safe place again.

AP/WWP

Late night television lost a true legend in 1992 when Johnny Carson retired after 30 years.

As Johnny Carson contemplated retirement, a succession of potential successors to his late-night throne passed through *The Tonight Show*. Carson finally named his recurring guest host Jay Leno as his replacement when Johnny retired in 1992. David Letterman, who was expecting to assume Carson's seat, and fed up with the competition within his own network, officially left NBC in 1993 for new digs at CBS.

For a few years, *The Late Show With David Letterman* would outdo Leno's new show in the ratings, as Leno struggled to fill Carson's giant shoes. When NBC replaced Letterman with former *Saturday Night Live* writer Conan O'Brien, the future seemed uncertain for Leno. But by 1995, his ratings were up.

There you have it, a wrap up of television talk shows throughout history. Perhaps you remember watching them yourself, but more likely than not, the names of the shows and the hosts who brought them into living rooms around the country sound off familiar bells. So read on to catch a flashback of some of the more memorable moments in television talk show history.

Memorable Moments In TV Talk Show History

For as long as talk shows have been on the air, they've had dedicated legions of fans who never miss an episode. And over the years, the shows have had their memorable moments. Some were great television, some were bad, and some were merely strange. But they were all moments that no fan or viewer will likely ever forget.

Wedding Bells For Tiny Tim
December 17, 1969

Herbert Khaury, better known to fans as Tiny Tim, made a name for himself in the 1960s with the novelty hit "Tiptoe Through The Tulips." Tim was certainly a character to stand out in a crowd, playing 1920s tunes in an age of hard rock. But people took even more notice when fans of late-night television tuned in to see the light hearted ukulele player get married.

As a recurring guest on such talk-variety shows as *The Tonight Show* and *Laugh-In*, Tiny Tim decided that, like a true performer, his wedding ought to be public. And public it was, as an audience of millions tuned in to *The Tonight Show* in 1969 to watch Tiny Tim exchange vows with the 17-year-old Miss Vicki Buddinger. Even though the marriage didn't last, Tim's unprecedented television nuptials made Johnny Carson's already popular spot the most-watched show of the evening.

Tiny Tim and Miss Vicki at their televised wedding.

Geraldo's Famous Brawl
November 3, 1988

AP/WWP

Geraldo Rivera's tendency to book controversial guests caught up with him in 1988.

Geraldo never hesitated to take on topics that other shows were afraid to touch. When tempers grew too hot to be contained between a group of teenage white supremacists and African-American activist Roy Innis, Innis and one of the white supremacists started engaging in an all-out brawl, a fight that didn't stop until an intervening Geraldo had a chair smashed across his face and a broken nose. The episode made headlines before it even went on the air, and the event single-handedly shot afternoon talk shows into the new era of "trash TV."

Oprah's Graphic Diet
November 15, 1988

Oprah Winfrey loves to share her experiences with her devoted television audience. In 1988, disappointed with her 180-pound frame, Oprah resolved to lose weight with the help of a liquid diet and vigorous exercise. After she had successfully slimmed down, she revealed her new svelte physique by prancing about in a tight turtleneck shirt and new size 10 jeans. Oprah then wheeled in a wagon loaded with 67 pounds of animal fat to show the audience how much weight she'd lost. "Not one single thing I have ever done has measured up to this kind of accomplishment," she said.

Madonna's Censored Interview
March 31, 1994

We all know the proverbial "material girl" for never hesitating to speak her mind on anything. When Madonna walked on David

Letterman's set, she was carrying a pair of her own underwear, which she gave to Dave. Right from the start, the interview was enough to shock the network's censors into overtime. Believe it or not, this is an actual transcript and Madonna's interview contained a whopping total of 13 obscenities:

Dave: What brings you . . .

Madonna: Incidentally, you are a sick f____. I don't know why I get so much s____.

Dave: You realize this is being broadcast, don't you?

Madonna: You're twisted.

Dave: Well, you can't be talking like that.

Madonna: What?

Dave: I said . . . oh, never mind . . . We're going to do a commercial and, uh, we are going to wash her mouth out with soap.

Madonna: And he's going to smell my underwear.

Drew Barrymore's Table Dance April 12, 1995

Believe it or not, Drew Barrymore once had a thing for a gap-toothed geek – *The Late Show's* David Letterman. "I've had a crush on him since I was seven," the young movie star explained. "I've never acted on my crush because each time I've met Dave, I've been heavily involved with someone else." Whether or not that's true, Dave got a regular eyeful of

David Letterman won't likely forget his 1995 birthday present from his not-so-secret admirer, Drew Barrymore.

Drew in 1995. In honor of the host's birthday, she jumped right up on his desk and gave Dave a spontaneous "table dance" before actually baring her breasts to him while her back was to the camera.

One look at the stunned host's face was enough to convince viewers that Dave really enjoys his job.

Rosie O'Donnell vs. Tom Selleck
May 19, 1999

When Tom Selleck appeared on *The Rosie O'Donnell Show*, he was expecting a simple interview, just an opportunity to plug his latest movie *The Love Letter*. He was wrong.

As a strong advocate of gun control, Rosie certainly wasn't going to let Tom go without taking issue with his active membership in the National Rifle Association. In the wake of the shootings at Columbine High School, she strongly criticized his involvement with the gun lobby.

Rosie: But you can't say that guns don't bear a responsibility . . . the NRA wouldn't say as a matter of compromise, 'we agree, assault weapons are not good?'"

Tom: I can't speak for the NRA.

Rosie: But you're their spokesperson, Tom, so you have to be responsible for what they say.

Tom Selleck certainly wasn't happy with having his views questioned on national television, and Rosie wanted to make an important political point. Their heated debate sparked a wave of viewer responses on both sides of the gun control issue, proving that talk show viewers certainly do care about the issues of the day.

Behind-The-Scenes With Today's Hottest TV Talk Show Hosts

When a TV talk show host steps into the spotlight on national television every night (or morning or afternoon), viewers tend to look at the entertainer in a certain way. They might see David Letterman as the sarcastic, wise-cracking character, or Craig Kilborn as the fraternity house clown.

But few fans know the real people behind these characters. They're everyday people, no different from the rest of us. So what exactly is it that catapulted Oprah Winfrey to fame and fortune, or put Jay Leno on the *Tonight Show* throne?

These profiles will be your window into the real lives, trials *and* triumphs of 24 of today's most famous – and – infamous talk show hosts. We've got all those folks who bring us historic interviews, zany comedy or profound advice – or even a bit of all three! You'll see the morning show hosts (Regis Philbin), the afternoon ringmasters (Ricki Lake) and the kings of the after-hours airwaves (Conan O'Brien). They are the guardians of the serious news (Charlie Rose, Larry King) and the lords of "trash TV" (Jenny Jones, Jerry Springer). We've even got the legends of late-night (Jay Leno, David Letterman) and the relative newcomers (Dr. Laura Schlessinger). No matter who you watch, what you watch or when you watch it, you're certain to find a favorite personality.

In each of the profiles, we'll answer your questions about the stars of talk. Where are they from? How did they break into show business? Were they ever in a movie? We've also included some personal information, such as marital status, and even a personal quote here and there. So sit back, relax and prepare to find out just who these people are, anyway!

AP/WWP

Joy Behar

The View

WHO IS JOY BEHAR ANYWAY? After years of therapy to learn to overcome performance anxiety, this former high school teacher, receptionist and unemployed stand-up comic has hit it big as one of the hosts on the morning talk show *The View*.

Birth Name
Josephine Victoria
Aquina Occhiuto

Birth Date
October 7, 1943

Birthplace
Brooklyn, New York

Marital Status
Single

Children
Eve

Pets
Max (Shitzu dog)
Benito Pussilini (cat)

The year was 1997 and Joy Behar had just gotten the biggest break of her career. She had been chosen to be one of the co-hosts on *The View*, a new morning talk show headed up by veteran newsperson, Barbara Walters. Joy exclaimed, "I can't believe I got this job. I'm ready to jump out of my brassiere."

This sort of no-holds-barred comedic honesty was honed on the comedy club circuit where Joy had performed her routine for years. But this natural performer did not get to *The View* the easy way!

The Head Of The Class

Joy began her career performing in front of an audience in junior high school classrooms where she taught English.

She had been married to college professor Joe Behar for 14 years and was a mother to their daughter, Eve. But in 1979, an ectopic pregnancy nearly killed her, an event that gave her the courage to follow her dream of becoming a comedian. "I realized you can just be dead," Joy remembers. Although she survived, her marriage did not. "We were going in different directions," she says. Joy and Joe divorced in 1981.

Oh, Joy!

Joy was employed as a receptionist for *Good Morning America*, where she secretly hoped to be "discovered." At night, she haunted the club circuit, but her fear of performing was intense. "I'd drive by comedy clubs and get nauseous," she said. So, she began psychotherapy to overcome her fear.

Joy (left), Fiona Hughes and Patrika Darbo share a hug and a congratulations after they recieved word of their Emmy nominations in 2000.

In 1983, Joy was fired from *Good Morning America* – for not always being nice to callers. Joy explained, "People would call and ask, 'Where's Joan Lunden?' I'd say, 'I don't know where Joan Lunden is.'"

On The Road

Without the safety net of a steady job, Joy sometimes performed her comedy routine six nights a week. She was starting to get laughs, but most of the money she took home was from her unemployment check. And with her schedule, she had to find someone to watch over Eve, who was then about 12. So Joy's parents helped out when she worked at night. "She was a good mother," Eve says today, "but, in the morning, I had to do everything."

Joy remembers that "it was very hard to make the leap from teaching to comedy." But she kept at it, and soon her talent began attracting serious attention. She was getting good reviews and the respect of her fellow comedians. "I had my eye on her in the '80s," said jokester Robert Klein, "I thought, 'This one is sharp.'"

Over the next 10 years, Joy was finally able to make a comfortable living using her humor – thanks to bit parts in movies, hosting a popular New York City talk-radio show and touring nationwide as a headliner in clubs and shows.

Long-term Commitment

Her love life has improved too. In 1982, Joy met high school math teacher, Steve Janowitz, who is seven years her junior. Although they have been together for almost 20 years, they don't plan on tying the knot. "I don't see the point of getting married," says Janowitz. "Joy probably

Cleaning Up!

Joy's autobiography, *Joy Shtick: or What Is the Existential Vacuum and Does It Come With Attachments?*, was published in 1999.

feels even stronger about that than I do." And Joy adds, "I have a gorgeous apartment, then he has to stick his two cents in about what pictures to hang up? I want a man in my life . . . but not in my house."

Those comments were made in 1997 and her sentiments have apparently not changed since Joy and Steve are still together and are still not married. Today, however, they share the apartment (which she owns) that is located on Manhattan's Upper East Side.

Joy Ride

Since her debut on *The View* in 1997, there's no question that Barbara Walters – who said that Joy's wry sense of humor and witty take on current events would help make the new talk show a hit – was right. *USA Today* has said that Joy "generally steals the show" and she's been nominated for a Daytime Emmy for each year that she's been a co-host on *The View*. But the executives at ABC weren't so sure originally. "The industry thought I was too 'New York' for people in middle America to identify with. It turns out they were wrong, and I'm glad about that – and I thank Barbara Walters for taking a chance on me," says Joy.

Joy has found success doing what comes naturally – saying what is on her mind, which often reflects the feelings of a lot of women across the country.

Joy (right) is joined by cancer patient Brenda Taylor (left) of Charleston, WV and other participants in a "Race For The Cure" event in 1999.

The Everett Collection

Jenny Jones

The Jenny Jones Show

WHO IS JENNY JONES ANYWAY? With a hard-luck life that some consider shocking and hard to imagine, while others consider it inspiring, TV diva and real-life survivor Jenny Jones has hadthe experiences that could be very compelling topics for *The Jenny Jones Show*.

Birth Name
Janina Stronski

Birth Date
June 7, 1946

Birthplace
Jerusalem

Resides
Chicago, Illinois

Marital Status
Single

Hobbies
Cooking, photography, sewing

Turn on the television, tune in to *The Jenny Jones Show*, and you will see Jenny Jones, the polished and professional interviewer and entertainer. She knows how to communicate to her guests and how to empathize with their problems. How does she do it?

Jenny explains it this way: "I am truly one of my guests. I come from dysfunctional. I could be one of the teens on (a *Jenny Jones Show* segment called) 'Out Of Control Teens.' My parents could be on 'I Survived An Affair.' I could also be on 'I Survived My Attacker' or 'Sibling Rivalry' because my sister and I went separate ways. I can relate to most people's problems. I was where they are." What an understatement!

From Bad To Worse

Born Janina Stronski, Jenny began life with the odds stacked against her. The child of Polish postwar refugees who moved to Canada when she was 2, Jenny had few role models as she was growing up. Both of her parents indulged in extramarital affairs, which led to their divorce before Jenny turned 12. Her mom – a binge drinker and diet pill-popper – verbally abused Jenny and her older sister. Consequently, Jenny's father gained custody of the girls but "it was not much of an improvement," she says. She was "shoplifting, drinking and necking with guys that we just picked up" and finally, quit school.

Escape To L.A.

Jenny's dream was to become a rock star. She had taught herself to play jazz drums and toured with her band. In 1964, she changed her name to Jenny Jones and arrived in Los Angeles. After working as hostess in a strip club, she moved to Las Vegas, formed an all-girl band and was discovered by Wayne Newton, who hired Jenny as a backup

AP/WWP

Jenny talks to the audience during a taping of
The Jenny Jones Show

singer. In one month, she was appointed Wayne's background vocal arranger. It had been during those years that Jenny learned she had another talent – comedy.

Pick Yourself Up . . .

By 1979, Jenny knew she wanted to do stand-up. But her troubled childhood and three failed marriages within a span of 10 years filled her with self-doubt. To boost her confidence, Jenny decided to get breast implants. And, after she went from an AA to a C cup, she felt that she could face the world – from the stage of comedy clubs. She performed her stand-up routine for five years and then, at the age of 40, Jenny finally got her big break. In 1986, she became the first woman ever to win the Comedy Grand Prize on *Star Search*. The prize brought acclaim and $100,000. Finally, she didn't have to worry about money.

. . . And Start All Over Again

But, "four years after *Star Search*," according to her publisher, "she'd lost it all – the money, the fame, the opportunities, the self-confidence. To save herself from financial ruin and career oblivion, Jenny developed *Girls' Night Out*, an irreverent for-women-only comedy show that's part stand-up comedy, part talk show, and part group therapy." The reaction to Jenny's cabaret act was extraordinary. It attracted record crowds and the show – and Jenny – got nationwide media coverage.

A spotlight on *20/20* caught the eye of a Warner Brothers executive who asked Jenny to star in her own TV talk show. *The Jenny Jones Show* first aired in 1991 and made TV history as the top-selling new first-run talk show.

But, Can She Keep The Clothes?

Does Jenny get to keep the clothes she wears on her show? "No," she says, "but if I really like something, I might accidentally get a pen mark on it, and then the show has to buy it."

Cuff Her

Jenny has been arrested for: attempting to enter the U.S. from Canada without the proper documents, shoplifting and attempting to carry a pistol through an airport safety checkpoint.

A Roller Coaster Ride

Throughout the early '90s, Jenny's show continued to be a phenomenal success. Her audience loved to watch the spunky host interview outrageous guests. But, in 1995, after a taping of a show on "secret same-sex crushes," a guest was killed by another guest who had confessed that he had feelings for him. The tragedy devastated Jenny. The victim's family filed a lawsuit against the show and a jury ultimately awarded the family $25 million in damages.

Although the lawsuit didn't hold Jenny personally responsible, many people did. Jenny found herself attacked in the media but Warner Brothers stood by her and, to this day, she claims. "If it were a man and a woman, no one would have had an issue."

A Better Time And Place

Jenny was persuaded by producer Denis McCallion, her long-time boyfriend, to write her autobiography in 1997. The most difficult parts for her was to revisit her relationship with her mother and to discuss the removal of her problematic breast implants. To the fans who love her, Jenny's struggle to overcome the trials and tragedies in her life is inspiring and gives them the courage to confront their own.

Jenny relaxes on the set of her show, *The Jenny Jones Show.*

The Everett Collection

Star Jones

The View

WHO IS STAR JONES ANYWAY? Some people call Star tough, aggressive and in-your-face. But this former prosecutor turned TV star says she's just a "Babe In Total Control of Herself."

Birth Name
Starlet Marie Jones

Birth Date
March 24, 1962

Birthplace
Badin, North Carolina

Resides
New York City

Marital Status
Single

Children
"My fulfillment does not require me to bring forth life."

Hobbies
Reading, listening to jazz

Star was born in 1962 in the little town of Badin, North Carolina. Her mother was the first to see that Star was special. "She had these big eyes and they just twinkled," mom Shirley told *Ebony* magazine. "They made me think of stars." And so she named her baby daughter Star.

Learning To Shine

Raised by two sets of grandparents while her mom and dad finished college, Star's strict upbringing taught her to value spirituality, hard work and personal excellence. "I come from people who believe that family is first and God has to play a part in your life, or your life means nothing," Star had once told *Ebony* reporter Kelly Starling.

> ## Move Over Imelda Marcos!
>
> By various accounts, Star owns between 300 and 500 pairs of shoes. She's admitted to owning 350, in a *PEOPLE* magazine on-line chat, and to having worn at least 300.

"My parents armed me with a feeling that I could accomplish anything and that they would always be there with love and support," Star said. "It's a great gift to give a child."

Star Quality

When Star was 6, her parents divorced and she moved with her mother and sister to Trenton, New Jersey. The family was living in public housing, but, even then, Star knew she was ultimately destined for big things.

Star decided to become a lawyer – at the tender age of 7. "I dreamed of being like F. Lee Bailey," she says. At this time, she began to show off her sense of style too. The fashionable Star loved to dress up in Mom's high heels to cheer for her school's teams in the dusty ball field.

Star celebrates with her co-hosts from *The View* – Barbara Walters, Joy Behar and Mededith Viera – for their Daytime Emmy nominations for Outstanding Talk Show Host and Outstanding Talk Show.

Career Highlights

Court TV (1991-1992)

NBC Nightly News
(1992-1995)

Jones & Jury (mid 1990s)

Today (1992-1995)

Inside Edition (1995-1997)

The View (1997-present)

Seeing the Light

Then in 1982, Star faced a huge challenge when doctors discovered a tumor in her thymus gland. "I was 20 years old and a doctor told me a tumor was choking the life out of me. He told me I had nine months to live."

But Star refused to accept this verdict. "I've never been the kind of person to accept someone else's opinion when it comes to my life," she said. Another doctor and surgery saved her life. "God kept me here for a purpose," Star says. "Maybe that's one of the reasons I decided to become a prosecutor. I wanted to fight the taking of a life."

A Star In The Courtroom . . .

Star attended the University of Houston Law School and passed the New York State Bar Exam on her first try – the one accomplishment she's most proud of. She went to work as an assistant district attorney in Brooklyn, New York, and quickly built an impressive record as a tough prosecutor. But destiny came calling – on the telephone. In 1991, a colleague asked her to fill in as a guest commentator on Court TV. The case was the William Kennedy Smith rape trial.

. . . And In The Newsroom

Star's Court TV commentary led to a guest spot on NBC's *Today* show. Then two months later, in 1992, she was offered a six-figure contract to become NBC's legal correspondent for *Today* and *Nightly News*. There, she covered

What Is Your Opinion?

In 1998, Star became a critically acclaimed best-selling author with the publication of her novel, *You Have To Stand For Something Or You'll Fall For Anything*.

some landmark cases – the Mike Tyson rape trial, the Rodney King's police brutality trial, and the trials of the Menendez brothers and Lorena Bobbit. Star's sky-rocketing popularity led to the creation of her very own TV show, *Jones & Jury*. In 1997, Star was selected by Barbara Walters to be one of the co-hosts for *The View*.

Heavenly Body

Star's elegant sense of style has also propelled her into the fashion arena. She wears a wig every day on *The View*, and in 1998, launched a line of wigs and hairpieces, "The Star Jones Collection." And, in 1999, she became spokesperson for "Salon Z" of Saks Fifth Avenue.

Inspiration

In spite of her absolutely fabulous success, Star has not forgotten what it is that's important in life. "I don't define success as sitting next to Barbara Walters and wearing designer evening gowns," she says. "Maybe there's some little girl out there who wants to be a lawyer and is being told she's no good. Maybe something I've said or done will pull someone out of a place of despair and help them go on. If that's what happens, I will feel I fulfilled my obligation to God."

Star relaxes in her dressing room on the set of *The View*.

AP/WWP

Craig
Kilborn

The Late Late Show

WHO IS CRAIG KILBORN ANYWAY? As the host of *The Late Late Show* on CBS, "Craiggers" asks guests the hard-hitting questions other hosts are afraid to ask, such as, "How does my hair look?"

Birth Name
Craig Kilborn

Birth Date
August 24, 1962

Birthplace
Kansas City, Missouri

Marital Status
Single (declines to name his current girlfriend)

Children
Jonathan

Comedic Inspirations
Johnny Carson, Bill Murray

Favorite Sport
Basketball

What is Craig Kilborn really like? Is he the arrogant "pretty boy" whose often off-color comments got him suspended from *The Daily Show*? Or is he the down-to-earth fellow whose self-deprecating humor achieves a humble dignity? Love him or hate him, Craig Kilborn's unique blend of attitude and absurdity has made him a star on the late night talk show scene.

Hoop Dreams

Even though he was born in Missouri, Craig grew up in Hastings, Minnesota. Tall as a child, Craig stood well over six feet by high school. He also stood out on the basketball court, where his size and natural ability made him a lifelong player – and die-hard fan – of the sport.

After high school, Craig accepted a basketball scholarship from Montana State University, where he majored in film and television. Although Craig played well in his three years on the team, Craig plays down his achievements, claiming that he led the Big Sky Conference in turnovers. Perhaps a future in the NBA wasn't in the cards for Craig after all and Craig sat out his senior year on the court to focus more on his academics. After graduating, he turned down a chance to play pro ball – in Luxembourg. "Dad always told me I'd never play in the NBA," Craig says, "so I'd better figure something else out."

Craig made his way to Los Angeles in the hopes of entering the other side of the sports business – broadcasting. He finally got his big chance at sportscasting when he found work as a play-by-play man for the Continental Basketball Association's Savannah Spirits franchise. After his tenure with the Spirits ended, Craig set out to find fame in California.

Wake Up With Craig!

In California, Craig tried his hand at a few odd jobs on the way to television. He now makes fun of his stint as a waiter in an

Professional wrestler The Rock gives Craig pointers in how to perform the "people's eyebrow."

Italian restaurant, stating "I came from Minnesota – I had no idea what pesto sauce was." Eventually, Craig began making a name for himself as a television sportscaster for stations in Santa Rosa and Monterey. The experience was enough to land him a job at ESPN. Craig found himself up in the wee hours anchoring the early morning *SportsCenter* desk. Rather than languish in an inhospitable time slot, Craig thrived, becoming well known for such quirky phrases as "Jumanji!" and "Do a little dance, make a little glove."

A Comedic Moment

Craig had become a favorite of sports junkies, but Doug Herzog, president of Comedy Central, sensed Craig had an even more far–reaching appeal, and Herzog was looking for an anchor to host an offbeat news program for his cable comedy station.

It didn't take long for *The Daily Show* to take off in the ratings. Craig, with his good looks and perfect hair, was an ideal "stereotypical" news anchor for the program. News reports written by the talented *Daily Show* staff amused viewers daily. and Craig even came up with some of his own material. His "Five Questions" segment, which quizzed celebrity guests and the "Moment For Us," which closed each episode, both became comedic standouts on the show.

Host vs. Writer

Despite the show's success, the creative disagreements between Craig and head writer Lizz Winstead almost brought the show crashing down. His racy comments about Winstead in an issue of

Craig's First Sidekick

Although Craig doesn't have a sidekick on his show, in his childhood attempts at comedy, he did – a ventriloquist's dummy he named Lenny Carr! Craig can still manage to speak without moving his lips, although, when he does, he has to call his favorite sport "vasketvall."

Esquire magazine resulted in a week's suspension for the host. Craig now admits, "I made a terrible mistake for which I am truly sorry." Winstead eventually left the network, but viewers were willing to accept Craig's apology.

Up All Night

Craig was considering leaving Comedy Central as well. After three years on *The Daily Show*, the big networks came calling, and CBS offered Craig the hosting duties of *The Late Late Show*. And Craig's decision to take the offer left it s mark. In place of departing host Tom Snyder, Craig brought a youthful edge. He also brought his "Five Questions" bit, the ownership of which was initially challenged by Comedy Central.

Despite Craig's image, his personal life remains a mystery. He has a young son, Jonathan, from a previous relationship, and has always refused to divulge Jonathan's mother's name. He also won't share information about his love life, declining to name his girlfriend.

With his late-night success, Craig seems poised to enter the world of superstardom. Despite what some viewers say, Craig's brand of comedy is anything but "frat boy" humor. He's more jocular than jock, and proves it every night as he pokes fun at himself.

Craig's first night as host of *The Late Late Show* found him flanked by model Heidi Klum and actor Bill Murray.

Image Direct

Larry King

Larry King Live

WHO IS LARRY KING ANYWAY? While the young King who was barely passing high school could have been voted the *least* likely to succeed, this much-married, once-arrested high school graduate is now one of the most popular, powerful and celebrated TV talk show hosts in the world.

Birth Name
Lawrence Harvey Zeiger

Birth Date
November 19, 1933

Birthplace
Brooklyn, New York

Resides
Washington, D.C.
Provo, Utah
(vacation home)

Marital Status
Married to Shawn
Southwick
(singer/infomercial host)

Children
Cannon, Chance, Kelly,
Chaia, Andy, Larry Jr.

Larry Zeiger grew up in Brooklyn, New York, the son of Russian Jewish immigrants. When he was only 9, his dad died of a heart attack and his mother was forced to go on welfare to support Larry and his younger brother. Larry endured rough times while always dreaming of becoming a radio announcer.

"When I was 5 years old," Larry recalls, "I would fantasize being a broadcaster. Always, in the back of my mind, I wanted to get into radio."

After high school, Larry worked as a truck driver for UPS and hung around radio stations in New York City, hoping for a break. An announcer at CBS told him to go to Miami and at age 23, Larry caught a bus south.

A New Name And A New Beginning

In Miami, Larry slept on an uncle's couch until a small station, WAHR, hired him in 1957. Soon, he got an on-air job as a morning disc jockey, plus newscasts and sports – for $55 a week.

Before Larry went on the air, the manager asked him to change his last name – Zeiger was too ethnic and too hard to spell. The manager choose the name "King" from a *Miami Herald* newspaper ad for King's Wholesale Liquors.

Larry turned on the mike and said, "Good morning, this is my first day ever on radio. All my life I wanted to be in radio , , , my name is Larry King. It's the first time I've ever said that name and I am scared to death. But I'm going to try to communicate." And Larry was never nervous on the air – again.

Larry discusses the possibility of a Donald Trump presidency with the business mogul and potential candidate in 1999.

Public Disgrace

Larry's radio show caught on, and then in 1960, he got his first TV show, *Miami Undercover*. His popularity kept on growing. But, in 1971, Larry was arrested for grand larceny – he allegedly stole $5,000 from a business partner. Although all charges were dropped, Larry was now deep in debt and no one wanted to hire him.

"I didn't handle money well," he says of those desperate years. "I was making $50,000 and living $80,000." Larry slowly rebuilt his career. By 1978, the scandal had blown over and Larry began broadcasting in Florida again.

Career Highlights

TELEVISION:
Larry King Live
(1985-present)

FILM:
Cameo appearances in over two dozen movies, including *The Contender* (2000), *Bulworth* (1998) and *The Exorcist III* (1990)

Changing History

Larry has set a lot of records. He's one of the best known broadcast personalities in the world. He's done over 40,000 interviews and has logged more radio time than any other announcer. "Larry King Live" was the first ever worldwide phone-in TV talk show and CNN's highest rated show.

In 1992, Ross Perot announced his presidential candidacy on "Larry King Live," another first. Larry's non-stop parade of celebrities have made him more popular than ever, with over 400 stations broadcasting his show.

Matters Of The Heart

Larry first marriage was to Frada Miller right after high school. The union was annulled shortly thereafter, and he has since gone on

From The Pen

King has written 11 books to date including the following: *Anything Goes!: What I've Learned from Pundits, Politicians, and Presidents* (2000), *Future Talk: Conversations about Tomorrow with Today's Most Provocative People* (1998) and *Powerful Prayers* (1998).

Awards

Larry has indeed become a huge success and has the awards to prove it. Some of his many honors include: his induction into the Broadcasters' Hall Of Fame in 1996 and a Star on the Hollywood Walk of Fame in 1997.

to tie the knot six more times. In between, there were several long-term relationships, including one with actress Angie Dickinson. In 1997, Larry married singer-model-TV host Shawn Southwick, 26 years his junior, at his hospital bedside on the eve of his most recent angioplasty surgery.

However, while his romantic heart was strong, his physical one was not. A weak heart that he probably inherited from his father and a life-long smoking habit caused Larry to suffer a number of heart attacks. He has since founded the Larry King Cardiac Foundation to financially assist others in need of cardiac surgery.

Living His Dream

Larry is thrilled by his incredible success. "I get to meet the most interesting people in the world and ask then anything I want," he's written. Although his latest contract was for $35 million, Larry's success is apparently not about the money.

Larry King is living his dream. "I'm having as much fun today as I did when I made $55 a week," he says. "Because it is as much fun – if you're a disc jockey in Biloxi, Mississippi, making a hundred dollars a week, you're having as good a time as me."

Larry proves that seven is a lucky number as he renews his vows with wife number seven, Shawn Southwick.

Corbis

Ricki
Lake

The Ricki Lake Show

WHO IS RICKI LAKE ANYWAY? Ricki Lake is the host of her own hit daytime talk show and has appeared in numerous roles for director John Waters' campy films. Her show's topics may have critics shaking their heads, but this talk maven is not afraid to showcase the issues that concern her Gen-X audience.

Birth Name
Ricki Pamela Lake

Birth Date
September 21, 1968

Birthplace
Hastings-on-Hudson,
New York

Resides
New York City

Marital Status
Married to Rob Sussman
(political illustrator)

Children
Milo Sebastian

Famous Friends
Debbie Gibson

A versatile performer, Ricki Lake has wowed audiences all over America with her many talents, including singing, acting and, of course, hosting a successful talk show.

A Star Is Born

Ricki was raised, along with her younger sister Jennifer, in New York's Westchester suburbs by her parents – Barry, a pharmacist and Jill, a homemaker.

In her teens, Ricki began to showcase her talent by singing in cabarets and clubs and auditioning for commercials and Broadway shows. She learned to play four instruments – the piano, clarinet, piccolo and flute. She starred in school plays and eventually decided to focus on her acting skills by attending the Professional Children's School in New York City. During this time, she made her television debut with a guest spot on the popular sitcom *Kate & Allie*.

After high school, Ricki attended Ithaca College but soon she was ready to call it quits and move to California to pursue her career. However, before she could pack her bags, her agent called with news of an audition for the John Waters' film, *Hairspray*. And it all began when she got the part of the overweight teenage daughter of transvestite, Divine, and became an immediate hit.

Don't Weigh Me Down

Ricki had always been heavyset, weighing about 200 pounds when she did *Hairspray*. When production of the movie ended, she put on even more weight, eventually reaching an estimated 250 pounds on her 5'4" frame. She told *PEOPLE* magazine that she

Ricki and husband Rob Sussman snuggle for the camera.

Career Highlights

TELEVISION:
China Beach (1989-1990)
The King of Queens
(2000-present)
The Ricki Lake Show
(1993-present)

FILM:
Hairspray (1988)
Mrs. Winterbourne (1996)

had a hat collection "because they were the only thing that fit me."

After appearing in various bit parts in both movies and television, including a recurring role on *China Beach*, the phone stopped ringing. Ricki's job opportunities had suddenly dried up. She even had to sell the Hollywood Hills home she purchased in 1989 just to make ends meet.

Ultimately, Ricki decided that there was something she wanted to lose – weight. Over the next three years she dropped almost 130 pounds through a vegetarian diet and a strict exercise regimen. She went down to a size 10 and trimmed to a size 8 for her role in the film *Mrs. Winterbourne* (1996).

Talk To Me!

It was in 1993 that Ricki wowed talk show producers during an audition by getting them to talk about themselves. "I have a natural curiosity when it comes to people," says Ricki. This was her big break. Ricki's new show was targeted at 18- to 34-year olds and it hit its mark. Its widespread appeal with young audiences eventually catapulted the show to #2 as far as number of viewers, just behind Oprah.

Soon, other talk shows hit the airwaves imitating Ricki's formula, but none could touch the original. That's not to say that the show did not have its critics. Many people were outraged by the controversial topics Ricki presented.

Everyone's A Critic

In response to Ricki's critics, show producers are candid, saying, "Our audience is more interested in dating than marriage. They like issues about teenage pregnancy and sexually transmitted diseases, topics that affect people their age." And Ricki's ability to get real people talking about real Generation-X issues is what makes her and her show a success.

Talk Show Hosts And The Men Who Love Them

Ricki first met Rob Sussman, a struggling artist, at a Halloween party in 1993 and it was love at first sight. The couple moved in together after only two weeks. Five months later, on March 26, 1994, they were married in Las Vegas – where Ricki's parents now live. Ricki described her wedding to *Time* magazine saying that "The chapel was tacky, and this woman minister who married us was really creepy."

The couple has since had to deal with the ups and downs of Ricki's success and Rob's career struggles. But they have overcome their hardships and begun to build their family. It was during a romantic trip to Paris that Ricki became pregnant. Milo Sebastian was born in March of 1997. The couple are expecting another child in the summer of 2001.

Shine On

Ricki's show has made her a household name but when it is over, she still hopes to go back to her acting career. An accomplished actress, Ricki has starred in over a dozen big screen and television films, as well as several off-Broadway shows.

Ricki now has a recurring role as the title character's sister on the CBS sitcom, *The King Of Queens* and there's no telling how far her star will rise.

Ricki shows that rubber balls and black vinyl make an irresistible combination.

AP/WWP

Queen Latifah

The Queen Latifah Show

WHO IS QUEEN LATIFAH ANYWAY? When she's not rapping or writing, this multi-talented musician, actor and author is also the host of *The Queen Latifah Show*.

Birth Name
Dana Owens

Birth Date
March 18, 1970

Birthplace
Newark, New Jersey

Marital Status
Single

Famous Friends
Rosie O' Donnell

Favorite TV Shows
Survivor, World's Scariest Police Chases,
Trauma: Life in the E.R.

Hobby
Motorcycle riding

Born Dana Owens, the future Queen Latifah grew up in New Jersey. Her mother Rita, a teacher, and father Lance, a police officer, divorced when Dana was young. However, they were always there for her. "My mother raised me, but my father was never far away," Queen Latifah told *Ebony* magazine in 1993. The close-knit family suffered a blow in 1992 when Latifah's brother Lance Jr. died in a tragic motorcycle accident. "His death changed my whole perspective on life. It made me want to live more," she revealed to *Ebony* magazine.

Queen For A Day

Latifah has certainly lived her life to the fullest. Before the accolades for her acting started, she was a young, hip-hop

Soulfully Single

Queen Latifah has always been single. So why does she wear a platinum ring on her left hand? Well, as she told the *Daily News* in 1996, "I'm married to myself . . . (a)nd when I meet the right man who can treat me as well as I treat myself, I will take this ring off and replace it with his."

rapper determined to make it in the music world. Queen Latifah's unique name came from a cousin who nicknamed Dana "Latifah," an Arabic word known for its gentle connotation. The "Queen" part was Dana's idea. While still a teenager, Queen Latifah recorded her first rap album, *All Hail The Queen*. That album was the first in a successful career that would include the albums *Nature Of A Sista*, *Black Reign* and *Order In The Court*, among others. In 1994, Queen Latifah won a Grammy Award for Best Rap Solo Performance for her song "U.N.I.T.Y."

Latifah Living Large

Having conquered the world of music, Latifah set her sights on acting. For five seasons, she graced the small screen as Khadijiah James on the long running comedy *Living Single*. Feature films were now calling, and, after minor roles in films such as *Jungle Fever*, *Hoodlum* and *Sphere*, Latifah was given the chance to shine as a star in the 1996 gritty bank heist drama *Set It Off*. Later in 1998, a highly acclaimed role in *Living Out Loud* followed.

While her professional career was a series of high notes, Latifah's personal life was about to

Queen Latifah and her mother Rita Owens address high school students in Latifah's hometown of Newark, New Jersey.

Career Highlights

TELEVISION:
Living Single
(1993-1997)
Mama Flora's Family
(1998)
The Queen Latifah Show
(1999-present)

FILM:
Jungle Fever (1991)
My Life (1993)
Hoodlum (1997)
Sphere (1998)
The Bone Collector (1999)

yield a series of lows. After enduring a horrifying carjacking in 1995, Latifah found herself in court twice in 1996. An arrest for assaulting a photographer, along with an arrest for possession of a loaded gun and marijuana, indicated Latifah's career was in danger of derailing. But Latifah rebounded, putting her life in order and racking up more professional successes including the popular 1999 book *Ladies First: Revelations Of A Strong Woman.*

Following In Rosie's Footsteps

Latifah got the idea to create a talk show from Rosie O'Donnell, who knew the Queen would make an ideal host. Rather than wallow in the "muck" on which the other talk shows thrive, Latifah's program mixed celebrity guests and "real life" segments. When a young overweight guest revealed that she dropped out of school because of the excessive taunting she received, Queen Latifah promised to personally escort the youngster back to school. Queen Latifah stood by her promise and came with the student to her first day of class at her new school.

Viewers have responded to Queen Latifah's compassion. As a result, her show has been one of the few survivors out of a crop of talk show casualties. The program has over one million viewers per episode, and, while it started slowly, it had gained steam over its first two seasons, and shows no signs of slowing down any time soon.

Surprise!

When Queen Latifah turned the big "30," her talk show became the site of a surprise 30th birthday party. Guests in attendance included her mother as well as several of her *Living Single* costars. Taped messages came from Chris Rock, Mike Meyers and Regis Philbin.

A Presidential Dream

Although Latifah has had many impressive guests visit her show, she says her dream guest would be Chelsea Clinton.

The Queen And Her Court

Guests on "Queen Latifah" have included everybody from Democratic presidential candidate Bill Bradley to controversial musician Puff Daddy. The Queen's stature in the music and acting communities makes her show a popular destination for both rappers and actors. Her handsome *Bone Collector* costar Denzel Washington even stopped by to set the host's heart aflutter. "He's much more handsome in person than he is on film, and he's a much nicer person than you can ever imagine," she told *Jet* magazine.

Queen Latifah isn't afraid to mix up serious topics with the occasional "mothers who party with their kids" or "from nerd to knockout" episodes. Just as Latifah's career has spanned several genres, her talk show has proved to be equally expansive and Latifah is not content to rest on her laurels. The Queen has used her clout to record public service announcements reminding youngsters to register to vote, a topic that she feels quite passionate about.

Queen Latifah interviews presidential hopeful Al Gore during the 2000 campaign.

AP/WWP

Jay
Leno

The Tonight Show With Jay Leno

WHO IS JAY LENO ANYWAY? Owner of one of the world's most famous chins – and host of America's comedy institution, *The Tonight Show* – Jay Leno keeps millions of viewers laughing into the late night hours with his "feel-good," goofy brand of humor.

Birth Name
James Douglas Muir Leno

Birth Date
April 28, 1950

Birthplace
New Rochelle, New York

Resides
Los Angeles, California

Education
B.A., Speech Therapy
Emerson College

Marital Status
Married to Mavis Leno
(writer)

Hobby
Collecting classic cars
and motorcycles

He's the man who made "Headlines," "Iron Jay" and "Mr. Brain" household names. He's the man who filled Johnny Carson's shoes and took on David Letterman for the late-night TV crown. He's Jay Leno, the energetic everyman of comedy, who is one of the most popular entertainers in show business.

Humble Beginnings

Jay actually grew up in Andover, Massachusetts, where he gained a reputation as a joker and prankster in school. One of Jay's earliest inspirations was George Carlin, a comic Jay admired because he "had a whole hour where he just talked about things he used to do in school – passing notes, throwing spitballs

Star Pupil

On one of his 5th grade report cards, Jay's teacher wrote: "If Jay spent as much time studying as he does trying to be a comedian, he'd be a big star."

. . . a lot of the things I did." To this day, Jay insists that comedy wasn't always in the cards. "I didn't always know I wanted to be a comedian – as a kid I had no idea. But I kept making up jokes and doing my little routines, and after a while, it finally hit me that that's what I wanted to do."

But Jay has always been determined. When he was rejected from Emerson College (he was mildly dyslexic), Jay camped outside the admissions office and refused to leave until the director let him in. So when he set his mind on comedy, there was no question that he would make it. Especially with his wife of over 20 years, Mavis, by his side (she not only tours with him, but is often his test subject for new material, "Honey, is this funny? Does this work?").

Filling Big Shoes

While Jay kept them rolling in nightclubs all over the country, he made the national spotlight in movies and as a guest on *Late*

AP/WWP

Flamboyant basketball star Dennis Rodman leaves Jay in stitches with a funny comment.

Career Highlights

TELEVISION:

The Tonight Show With Jay
Leno (1993-present)
The Simpsons, voice (1998)
South Park, voice (1998)

FILM:

Wayne's World 2 (1993)
The Flintstones (1994)
Contact (1997)
Wag the Dog (1998)

Night With David Letterman. But Jay's ticket to fame was really as a regular guest host of *The Tonight Show With Johnny Carson*, beginning in 1987. Actually, Leno made his first appearance on Carson's show as a guest 10 years earlier. Jay's "up-and-at-them" attitude threw him into the thick of things: "I saw a comic on T*he Tonight Show* who I thought was terrible. The next day I got a plane to California. Didn't pack, just left. I think it's good to back yourself into a corner, because if you leave yourself any options, you'll take them. If you have no options but success, you'll hustle more."

It was that hustle that earned Jay a place in the big chair of *The Tonight Show* when Johnny Carson retired in 1992. Late night television fans will never forget the media frenzy when Jay was chosen over another NBC talk show favorite, David Letterman, who was touted as Carson's heir apparent. In 1993, Jay and Dave went head-to-head when Letterman took his show to network rival CBS. And the late night ratings war was on!

Leno is philosophical about his rivalry with Letterman: "These shows are not the divine right of kings. It [the crown] belongs to whomever works the hardest. I just try to do better than the other person." Jay has proven himself a tireless worker and has been called (even by Letterman!) the hardest-working man in show business.

Jay Leno: Wrestling Legend!

When mild-mannered Jay and "Hollywood" Hogan traded verbal pot shots in 1998, it was only a matter of time before the two men would square off in the ring! With Diamond Dallas Page and band leader Kevin Eubanks in his corner, Jay put a whuppin' on Hogan and evil promoter Eric Bischoff at World Championship Wrestling's *Road Wild* pay-per-view event.

More To Life Than Comedy

But there's more to Jay's world than comedy. One of his greatest passions is collecting classic cars and motorcycles. One of his greatest thrills was being invited to drive the pace car at the Indianapolis 500 in 1999. His reaction when offered the opportunity? "Yeeessss! Yes, I'm very interested. How much do I have to pay you?"

A Star On The Rise (And On The Sidewalk)

Away from the cameras, Leno is "a regular guy." For Jay, life is just a question of simplicity and balance: "If you think of life as like a big pie, you can try to hold the whole pie and kill yourself trying to keep it, or you can slice it up and give some to the people around you, and you still have plenty left for yourself."

On April 27, 2000, Jay earned a great honor by getting his own star on the Hollywood Walk of Fame. Best of all, he's contracted to stay with *The Tonight Show* through 2005 – guaranteeing the hard-working, hard-laughing Leno will keep America in stitches.

Jay waves from behind the wheel of a funky car that is part of the Disneyland Autopia ride.

Paul J. Richards/Corbis

David
Letterman

The Late Show With David Letterman

WHO IS DAVID LETTERMAN ANYWAY? He is the irreverent, spontaneous king of late night television, famous for his show's "Top Ten Lists," "Stupid Pet and Human Tricks" and a sarcastic but endearing style of interviewing on his show, *The Late Show With David Letterman,* on CBS.

Birth Name
David Michael Letterman

Birth Date
April 12, 1947

Birthplace
Indianapolis, Indiana

Resides
New Canaan, Connecticut

Education
Ball State University

Marital Status
Single

Children
None

For nearly two decades, David Letterman's humor has caused people to go to sleep with a smile on their faces. Why? He welcomes his guests with a hug and a private remark and then interrupts, pries into their personal life and calls them names. He hands out corny prizes such as light bulbs and canned hams to his studio audiences. What's the real story behind this late night show host who has referred to himself as a "gap-toothed monkey boy?"

Cloudy With A Chance Of Ham

Although his quirky humor was evident as he grew up, Dave's overwhelming shyness was rivaled by the fact that he, by his own admission, "looked like a duck."

A Canine Spare?

Suspicions that the antics on Letterman's show are rehearsed were quelled when one of his guests on "Stupid Pet Tricks" proceeded to use his pet dog as a bowling ball, much to Dave's great distress.

This did not interfere with Dave's dream of someday hosting a television show. After graduating from college with a broadcasting degree and marrying his college sweetheart in 1969, Dave was ready for television. At an Indianapolis station, where he did nearly everything from hosting movies to broadcasting the weather, he first got himself into trouble with the management by congratulating a tropical storm on being upgraded to hurricane status! He also claimed – on the air – that Indianapolis was being pelted by "hailstones the size of canned hams."

His Big Break

Leaving Indianapolis in 1975, Dave made his way to Los Angeles where his edgy style was welcomed at The Comedy Store, a nightclub that features stand-up comedians. After seven years of

AP/WWP

Dave listens intently as Minnesota Governor Jesse Ventura makes a point on the set of *The Late Show With David Letterman*.

Career Highlights

TELEVISION:
Debut on The Tonight
Show (1978)
The David Letterman
Show (1980)
Late Night With David
Letterman (1982-93)
The Late Show With
David Letterman
(1993-present)

marriage, Dave and his wife divorced in 1977 because "we'd just gotten married too young." He began to live the life of a single guy in Hollywood, an experience that "produced more anxieties than pleasures" for Dave. While performing at The Comedy Store, however, he met Merrill Markoe, a fellow comedian. They started dating and working together – Merrill, the writer, gave all of her best jokes to Dave, the performer.

Dave's comedic performances on Mary Tyler Moore's variety show, *Mary*, put him in front of the camera but his big break – an appearance with Johnny Carson on *The Tonight Show* – eventually turned into guest-hosting spots in Carson's absence. The short-lived *The David Letterman Show*, a 90-minute morning program, served as a prototype for *Late Night With David Letterman,* which premiered on NBC in 1982. According to Dave, the early success of the show was due to its head writer, Merrill Markoe, Dave's longtime girlfriend. But they "paid the price for working together" and eventually the relationship ended.

Was That Supposed To Happen?

Dave's spontaneous personality gave his show a spark and a feeling of irreverent fun. Dave's extreme sarcasm, however, sometimes got the better of him. Shirley MacLaine almost punched him for calling her "totally nuts." And some people have criticized Dave for his interviewing style, but he's always defended himself by pointing out that he "wasn't hired to be a great interviewer. This is supposed to be a comedy show."

When Dave was passed over to host *The Tonight Show* when Johnny Carson retired, Dave retooled his program and joined CBS with *The Late Show With David Letterman*. He used his popular acts – the "Top Ten List" and "The Stupid Pet and Human Tricks"

– and brought along his sidekick and musical director, Paul Shaffer, who had been with Dave since the debut of *Late Night* in 1982.

Long-running jokes, such as Dave's penchant for fast cars (resulting in a number of speeding tickets from the Connecticut state police), contribute to his appeal. When he was summoned for jury duty recently, Dave kept viewers up to date on his futile attempts to fulfill his civic duty.

"I'm Just A Kid Trying To Make A Living"

Dave's willingness to laugh at everything – including himself – has put his show in the top spot over the years. When Dave returned to his show in February 2000, after undergoing emergency quintuple bypass heart surgery, he was able to turn a life-threatening condition into an opportunity for telling some jokes. "'Bypass surgery' is when doctors surgically create new blood flow to your heart," he quipped on his show. "A 'bypass' is what happened to me when I didn't get *The Tonight Show*."

But, it wasn't until Dave bent over and touched his toes – one of his pre-monologue rituals – that Paul Shaffer and the rest of the 12 million viewers watching that night knew that "everything was going to be all right."

Dave gets some driving pointers from race car driver Bryan Herta.

Nick Elgar/Image Direct

Lisa
Ling

The View

WHO IS LISA LING ANYWAY? As *The View's* resident "Gen-Xer," Lisa Ling brings a twenty-something sensibility to the daily forum, which also includes famous co-hosts Barbara Walters, Meredith Vieira, Star Jones and Joy Behar.

Birth Name
Lisa Ling

Birth Date
August 30, 1973

Birthplace
Sacramento, California

Resides
New York City

Marital Status
Single

Hobby
Tae-Bo

Although Lisa Ling is not yet 30, she has built an impressive resume that rivals those of many television news veterans. As a young Asian-American in a field dominated by Caucasians, Lisa is able to give voice to issues that are often overlooked by the traditional news media.

A Whiz Kid Remembers

At age 16, when other children are dreaming of getting their driver's license, Lisa was hosting Sacramento's *Scratch*, the first news magazine aimed at teenagers. That job led to greater exposure on *Channel One*, a national news program which is seen by over 8 million school children each day. For *Channel One*, Lisa filed several fearless reports from Iraq and Vietnam, as well as war-torn Yugoslavia and Afghanistan. Although war reporting can be scary for a young broadcaster, Lisa knew she was performing an important duty. "The people who live there have to endure these horrific situations on a daily basis. If I can somehow convey their life experiences in even the most remote way, I feel proud," she explained to *The Houston Chronicle*. Lisa also found work producing documentaries for PBS affiliates. These documentaries ranged in subject matter from the life of the Dalai Lama to Lisa's own cousin Ali, who waged a battle with liver cancer.

The View From The Top

Lisa's big break came when she became one of eight candidates vying to replace the departing Debbie Matenopoulos on

AP/WWP

Celebrating New York's love of baseball, Barbara Walters tries on a rubber baseball mask as Lisa, her *The View* co-host, looks on in amusement.

ABC's popular morning show, *The View*. Her competition included Colin Powell's daughter Anne and Rachel Campos, best known for her season on MTV's *The Real World*. In the end, Lisa was the best match with her prospective costars. "This is a program about chemistry, and Lisa just worked. She's proven she can do an interview," said Barbara Walters to the *New York Daily News*.

The View gives Lisa an opportunity to talk about world news one minute and engage in relationship discussions or cutting-edge workouts the next. "I can still be an insightful person and do butt-tightening exercises," she told *PEOPLE* magazine.

Her Weekend Job

Recently, Lisa began to stretch her focus beyond *The View*. She is a weekly contributor to the magazine *USA Weekend*, applying her opinion and perspective to a wide variety of world and cultural topics.

But not to worry, the young talk show host isn't planning to leave *The View* any time soon. However, she does sometimes miss the excitement of reporting. "On one hand, I want to go back and hit the war zones and do some crazy reporting," Lisa told one journalist. "On the other hand, I'm pushing 30 [and] I'm ready to crank out a few kids."

Old Navy, New Critics

When Lisa starred in two Old Navy television commercials, she was surprised at the hostility the ads generated within the Asian community. Although Lisa took the job because she felt that it was empowering to minorities, her critics saw it quite differently.

"The Asian-American community saw it as me being materialistic and selling out to Old Navy. I was even getting blasted in online chat rooms for not having an Asian man in the commercial," she said.

A Voice To Be Heard

Being criticized by fellow Asian-Americans came as something of a surprise to Lisa, who has always been a vocal supporter for the increased presence of Asian-Americans in the media. "Asians are only put on the spotlight for violating human rights or stealing nuclear secrets. It conveys the wrong associations to the general public," she told students in a speech at Duke University.

In addition to championing the causes of minorities, Lisa is involved in charitable work. She is an active voice in the fight against pediatric cancer, and plans to run in the Boston Marathon as a tribute to her cousin's memory. "My point isn't to actually break any records. I will run, walk or crawl across that finish line."

Lisa's determination in work and life has helped her succeed where other young voices have failed. Now comfortably settled into her role on daytime television, the view couldn't be any brighter.

AP/WWP

Reporting from *Channel One*, Lisa's reports reached 8 million students in classrooms across the country.

Pacha/Corbis

Bill
Maher

Politically Incorrect

WHO IS BILL MAHER ANYWAY? Whether you love or hate him, it's impossible to ignore Bill Maher. As host of the funny and controversial *Politically Incorrect* on ABC, Bill puts a sarcastic and irreverent spin on current events with his trademark wit.

Birth Name
William Maher, Jr.

Birth Date
January 20, 1956

Birthplace
Manhattan (grew up in
River Vale, New Jersey)

Resides
Los Angeles, California

Education
B.A., English,
Cornell (1978)

Marital Status
"I'm single and
priced to move!"

In a recent interview, Bill Maher talked about one of his inspirations. "I always liked Dean Martin," said Bill. "I liked all the Rat Pack guys because they were politically incorrect long before the term was invented." After 20 years of acidic comedy, including eight as host of *Politically Incorrect*, Maher continues to do that famous label justice!

From New York to L.A.

Long before he became host of one of the most talked-about talk shows in the country, Bill was a stand-up comedian. He began his comedy career in the late 1970s during his college years (although Bill says he knew he wanted to be a comedian since he was 10 years old!).

Serious About Animal Rights

One of the social issues Bill takes very seriously is animal rights. As a celebrity spokesperson for PETA (People for the Ethical Treatment of Animals), he has taken on many causes. On the official *Politically Incorrect* web site, Bill notes, "I love animals. I'm not crazy about people. I will do anything for animals."

Bill started making a national name for himself and made regular appearances on *The Tonight Show With Johnny Carson* and *Late Night With David Letterman* throughout the 1980s. Bill also landed parts in several movies and television shows, and he eventually moved to Los Angeles.

Politically Incorrect and Proud Of It

Beneath Bill's deceptively laid-back exterior lurks a sharp and sarcastic wit. Whether it's on stage or on network television, Bill's verbal sword is always sharp and quick. It's that "no B.S." attitude that rubs many people the wrong way. Over the years, Bill's caustic comments have earned criticism from political pundits, religious groups, social activists and many others. But much of the

APWWP

Most guests of Bill's show, *Politically Incorrect*, are invited, but Darrin Farrow, seen here shaking hands with Bill, won his place on stage with an on-line charity auction bid of $47,000.

Career Highlights

TELEVISION:
Politically Incorrect
(1993-present)
The Larry Sanders Show
(1997)
Snoops (1999)
Spin City (1999)
FILM:
Primary Colors (1998)
EDtv (1999)
Tomcats (2001)

furor surrounding Bill has less to do with him than the lively debates on *Politically Incorrect*, a show Bill describes as "*The McLaughlin Group* on acid."

Moses And Xena?

Bill launched the show in 1993 on cable television's Comedy Central. The combination of his insightful humor and the show's unique format – drawing together four famous people to hash out a controversy – was a recipe for success.

Every topic was fair game on *Politically Incorrect*. Nowhere else could you see Marilyn Manson, James Carville, Tony Danza, Robert Reich, Charlton Heston and Lucy Lawless kick around controversial topics! In 1997, Bill brought his show to an even bigger national audience when *Politically Incorrect* was picked up by ABC and given a late-night time slot.

Cynicism And What It Can Do For You

Bill doesn't want to see that sort of hostility on his show, but it's clear that *Politically Incorrect* takes its smart and sarcastic tone from its host. In addition to being very intelligent, he's also a critic of American culture and revels in his trademark cynicism. In Bill's words, "I think we have to get more cynical, because we're too stupid; we're too naive; we're too easily sold to; we're too easily scared by the people who sell us products. And one of those products is politics, and politicians."

Among his outspoken stances is his position that people should abandon voting for Republicans or

Beep, Beep, Beep

Do Bill's guests always tell the truth? It's probably a good idea! Bill says, "That's the one thing that will get me going – my B.S. radar goes up if I hear a lie, and I'll call people on it. But as long as you tell the truth here about whatever it is, we're cool."

Combat Pay?

In 1997, Bill was a contestant on Alan Thicke's *Pictionary*, along with former *C.H.i.P.s* star Erik Estrada. When Erik won the game, he threw up his hands – and whacked Bill in the nose, knocking him out cold! A few minutes later, Bill recovered and the show continued.

Democrats. "Remember," Bill once quipped, "if you don't choose between two nearly identical white Christian businessmen, you'll lose your freedom."

His non-conformist, anti-establishment stance has riled up many people but it also has endeared Bill to a loyal fanbase, which he has described as "a small but very rabid following . . . A little army of 'politically incorrect' people."

The Right Bill

For Bill, being outspoken is a matter of having a clear idea of what's wrong and what's right with the country. He certainly takes a dim view of America's mass market culture. Many people categorize him as a liberal, a Democrat or another less gracious descriptive noun! But Bill insists he's just saying what he thinks is right and leaves the categorizing to others.

As for his show, Bill does not expect it to change the world. But when it's at its best, *Politically Incorrect* is informative and most of all, fun. "It's more fun when people argue," Bill once said. And with his peculiar take on the world, fans can look forward to a lot more fun in the future!

Frank Micelotta/Image Direct

Bill appears on stage during the 51st Annual Emmy Awards in 1999.

AP/WWP

Dennis
Miller

Dennis Miller Live

WHO IS DENNIS MILLER ANYWAY? He's HBO's late night king, who uses his sardonic wit and hefty vocabulary to give his opinion on the news. Dennis is perhaps best known for his work on *Saturday Night Live* and can be seen frequently advertising beer, cars and long distance phone service.

Birth Name
Dennis Miller

Birth Date
November 3, 1953

Birthplace
Pittsburgh, Pennsylvania

Resides
Santa Barbara, California

Marital Status
Married to Ali Epsley
(former model)

Children
Holden, Marlon

Comedic Influence
Richard Belzer

It's hard to turn on the television and *not* see Dennis Miller these days. From ad spots to football and late night monologues, our old friend from *Saturday Night Live* has ignored the critics and created his own HBO talk show.

Growing Up Dennis

While growing up in Pittsburgh, Pennsylvania to parents who didn't stay married long, Dennis was just an average kid. He discovered his talent for making people laugh during his sophomore year in high school when a muttered disparaging comment about his teacher got the high school football star chuckling. Unlike other comedians' stories, however, Dennis didn't drop his school books for a microphone and some dingy barroom

Boo?

In an effort to entertain the neighborhood kids one Halloween, Dennis "dug this shallow hole, set up a fake cemetery, dressed up like a ghoul and I popped out and went, 'AAAARGH!' It took me hours to get it together, and I'm eating dirt . . . and every kid just said, 'Hey Mr. Miller, how ya doin'?' It wasn't even a millisecond of terror."

stage – he wasn't much of a rebel. Dennis finished high school and completed his education at nearby Point Park College. What did he major in? Journalism – a course of study that didn't prepare him for the work he'd do directly after college, but it certainly came in handy when he was sitting behind a desk at *Saturday Night Live* doing the "Weekend Update."

Extra! Extra!

Apparently, Dennis didn't realize that journalists get paid according to the length of what they write, and this discovery caused him to think twice about his chosen career path. And as much as he wanted to look as "cool" as Robert Redford did in *All The President's Men*, he never worked at a newspaper, never carried a press pass.

Instead he took the typical odd jobs – a storm window salesman, a grocery store clerk – until one night at a local bar, he saw a horrible stand-up act and knew he could do it better. After Dennis promised the owner of the establishment that he would fill the bar with his friends if he could work the crowd, Dennis took the stage and found his destiny.

Dennis attempts to return a volley during a celebrity tennis match.

Lorne Michaels, creator of *Saturday Night Live*, found Dennis on a Los Angeles stage doing stand up routines and hired him to join the 1985 cast of *Saturday Night Live*. After saying "I'm outta here!" to his stand-up career, Dennis spent six years behind the desk of "Weekend Update," feverously scribbling on his notes to close each "broadcast." However, Dennis took his show on the road after six seasons, performing live from New York. He hosted awards shows, starred in Miller beer commercials and worked on his stand-up routines until he was offered a late night talk show in 1992 which aired opposite Jay Leno's show.

Here Today, Gone Next Week!

Dennis wasn't on the air for too long, especially after rumors of numerous disagreements between Jay and Dennis. Was Dennis upset about the cancellation? "The key is how you handle it. If you do it with a suitable degree of aplomb, they let you back in. If you . . . bemoan your fate . . . you're out. So you just shut up and say, 'Well, I'll get 'em next time.'" And "get 'em," he did, with three Emmy wins for his late night show, *Dennis Miller Live*, which debuted in 1994.

Live & Kickin'

Dennis Miller Live is the perfect forum for the sarcastic comedian. He rants and raves about the political system, discusses cultural phenomenons and even throws in a bit of a "Weekend Update"-esque newscast after taking calls from viewers. Sometimes his comedy,

Are You Ready For Some Encyclopedias?

He may have cleaned up his act for *Monday Night Football*, but Dennis did not leave his trademark obscure references behind. Some viewers may not catch all of Dennis's insightful dialogue, which is why *Britannica.com* developed the "Annotated Dennis Miller" to explain some of the commentator's often obscure and witty remarks.

and his offbeat literary and historical references, might leave viewers scratching their heads and running for the dictionary, but it's all part of his personality. Dennis says whatever he wants, but makes sure to qualify it all with his signature statement, "But that's just my opinion. I could be wrong." Yet, somehow, we get the feeling that he doesn't think he is.

Anything For A Laugh!

Dennis has been a late night success for most of his 15 years on air, doing sheer political comedy and commentary. But, Dennis, what do you know about football? In an effort to spice up the *Monday Night Football* commentary, Dennis cleaned up his language and joined the talking heads as a lively sportscaster for the 2000 season. Many thought he'd never make it – after all, what does a comedian know about football? Enough to get called back for a second year, apparently!

Family Man

He may be adored by millions, but what's really important to Dennis is his family. In fact, he named his company "Happy Family Productions." Married to former model Ali Epsley since 1988, Dennis and his wife are raising their two sons in Santa Barbara, California. What does his success mean to him? "Absolutely nothing. What means something is having a wife and kids, and if you can keep that together, that really means something."

Frank Micelotta/Image Direct

Dennis at the microphone
during the *GQ* "Men of the Year Awards."

AP/WWP

Conan
O'Brien

*Late Night With
Conan O'Brien*

WHO IS CONAN O'BRIEN ANYWAY? Conan is the outrageous host of NBC's *Late Night*, with a penchant for licking and growling at guests, while engaging in scathing monologues and unusual sketches. What does Conan do best? He makes insomnia entertaining.

Birth Name
Conan Christopher O'Brien

Birth Date
April 18, 1963

Birthplace
Brookline, Massachusetts

Resides
New York City

Education
B.A., Literature and History, Harvard (1985)

Marital Status
Single

Hobby
Collects guitars

When he climbed behind the *Late Night* desk to replace David Letterman in 1993, no one recognized him. The tall, lanky, redhead who jumped in front of the audience to deliver his first of many opening comedic monologues was a mystery to many. But people had been laughing at Conan for years, and they just didn't know it.

Finding His Roots

Conan's parents, Ruth and Thomas O'Brien, raised six children in Brookline, Massachusetts, a suburb of Boston. His Irish-Catholic upbringing is what gives Conan the base for much of his comedic material and it also fuels his self-deprecating humor – as does his height.

What Does It Spell? Conan!

Conan became late night's heartthrob, and his "adorability" status was recently immortalized on the pop culture scene. In the 2001 hit movie *Sugar & Spice*, a witty flick about five cheerleaders-turned-bank robbers, one of them is obsessed with Conan and even imagines his face on others actors' bodies.

Growing up – *way* up to 6'4" – was mildly traumatic for the young Conan, whose height and shock of red hair made him slightly awkward through high school. He describes his adolescent self as a "crane galumphing down the hall. A crane with weird hair, bad skin and Clearasil. Big enough for basketball but lousy at it . . ." The sense of humor Conan developed in high school certainly took him much farther than the basketball court, though he admits to using his wit mostly just to impress girls in those days.

Second In Class Comic

Cambridge was in Conan's backyard for much of his life, so it's no surprise that he spent four years roaming the elite campus of Harvard. A bit of an intellectual, Conan graduated magna cum laude in 1985 with degrees in both literature and history.

As if that's not accomplishment enough, Conan became only the second student in Harvard's history to serve for two years in a row as editor and writer for the renowned humor journal, *The*

Conan takes his routine to the public.

Harvard Lampoon. This comedic experience served him well after college on a little comedy show known as *Saturday Night Live*!

Career Highlights

TELEVISION:
Not Necessarily The
News, writer (1985)
Saturday Night Live
writer, (1988-1991)
The Simpsons, writer,
(1991-1993)
Late Night With Conan
O'Brien (1993-present)

From 1988 to 1991, Conan wrote many well-known sketches for *Saturday Night Live*, including "Mr. Short-Term Memory," which featured Tom Hanks and Phil Hartman. He also acted in a few skits, too. You may remember Conan in the "Irish Drinking Songs" skit and he was the doorman for the "Five Timers Club."

Homer Says . . .

Conan's favorite episode of *The Simpsons* is "Marge vs. The Monorail." Why? Because he wrote it! Conan left *Saturday Night Live* in 1991 to pair up with Matt Groening, creator of FOX's hit show, *The Simpsons*. Probably one of the most "animated" times in Conan's career, his scathing social commentary and understated humor came to the fore when he was putting words in Homer Simpson's mouth.

But when David Letterman left NBC and a late night time slot opened up, the network knew who would be perfect to fill his spot. However, although he had a fabulous band, The Max Weinberg Seven, and calm straight-man Andy Richter, Conan's show took a few years to catch on. NBC and the viewers just didn't think he was funny. His contract was renewed in 13 week periods, and was even cancelled at one point. Still, Conan never missed a show, because he and his cohort Andy were the only two on the NBC roster who could fill the 12:30 time slot.

His Trusty Taurus

Conan's not the type of guy to let fame go to his head. For years after he had gained a national audience, Conan continued to drive to work every day in his 1992 Ford Taurus. "It's a good car. It's the car I had when I got the job," Conan

Kudos

For his writing on *Saturday Night Live*, Conan received an Emmy for Outstanding Writing in a Comedy or Variety Series (1989).

In the beginning, Conan did find it difficult to fill David Letterman's shoes (even though they are both about the same height). Conan attributes this to their different comedic styles. "You never see me going up and talking to normal Joe on the street," Conan says. "My idea is more about creating a fake, cartoony world and playing with that."

explains. "This is proof that I haven't become a jerk. Yeah, right. I've become a jerk, but I'm disguising it with the fact that I still drive a Ford Taurus." Though he still keeps his Taurus in Connecticut, Conan treated himself to a Land Rover when his comedic style and interviewing prowess improved enough for NBC to sign his contract for five years.

A Growl & A Joke!

In 2000, Andy Richter left the show to pursue other creative interests. But Conan continues to make audiences laugh, often pulling band leader Max Weinberg into the mix.

Conan may be single, but he might not stay that way for long, considering that he was voted among *PEOPLE* magazine's 100 "most eligible bachelors" in 2000. He has dated *Friends* star Lisa Kudrow (they used to do improv together before either landed network backing) and Lynn Kaplan, a booking agent on *Late Night*. Watch out for this one ladies, he growls!

Actor Ben Affleck anticipating a question from Conan.

AP/WWP

AP/WWP

Rosie
O'Donnell

*The Rosie O'Donnell
Show*

WHO IS ROSIE O'DONNELL ANYWAY? She's "The Queen of Nice," the energetic host of the popular daytime variety show, *The Rosie O'Donnell Show*. Rosie's outrageous humor and no-nonsense personality has made her a talk show favorite since 1996.

Birth Name
Roseanne O'Donnell

Birth Date
March 21, 1962

Birthplace
Commack, New York

Marital Status
Single

Political Affiliation
Democrat

Famous Friends
Madonna
Melanie Griffith

When you turn on the TV to watch Rosie O'Donnell yuk it up with the likes of Tom Hanks, Winona Ryder and Tom Cruise (whom Rosie refers to as her "boyfriend!") on *The Rosie O'Donnell Show*, you're watching a genuine Hollywood fan.

A Tough Childhood

Ask Rosie about her childhood and she'll probably start with the death of her mother. Her mom was only 39 when she died of breast cancer when Rosie was 10. She was the middle of five children raised in an Irish-Catholic household on Long Island. Her father took his wife's death hard and began to withdraw emotionally from the family. "There were five small children and an emotionally distant father," Rosie once explained. "We sort of took care of ourselves." At that time, television became a big part of Rosie's life and she was particularly fond of *The Merv Griffin Show* and other talk shows.

College and Comedy

It was during her high school years, at age 16, that Rosie put together her first comedy routine. After graduation, Rosie went to Dickinson College in Pennsylvania and then to Boston University, but the comedy bug wouldn't go away. This high school class president eventually left school and devoted her time to her budding comedy career.

During the mid 1990s, Rosie's comedic talent got national attention when she appeared on Ed McMahon's *Star Search* a whopping five times – and won each time!

With her stand-up career rolling and a regular television role on Nell Carter's *Gimme A Break* in her back pocket, Rosie went on to produce and host a comedy show on VH-1 called *Stand Up Spotlight*. Rosie made several film appearances before landing the job that

Rosie, on Broadway, in *Seussical* the musical.

Career Highlights

TELEVISION:

The Rosie O'Donnell Show (1996-present)
Spin City (1997)
Blue's Clues (1998)
Ally McBeal (1999)

FILM:

A League of Their Own (1992)
Exit To Eden (1994)
The Flintstones (1994)
Wide Awake (1998)
Tarzan, voice (1999)

she could only have dreamed of as a kid: hosting her own entertainment show!

Let The Koosh Balls Fly!

Loyal fans of *The Rosie O'Donnell Show* know that she just loves to chat, to throw Koosh balls at the audience and to talk about the entertainment world – just like an everyday fan. "I don't think I'm trying to save TV, or be the antithesis of sleaze TV shows," Rosie commented in a 1997 interview. "I'm just trying to do Merv Griffin for the '90s, and I do genuinely have an appreciation of celebrities, of talent, of musicals."

Rosie always keeps her show comfortable and loose and members of the audience can look forward to a carton of milk and a package of snack cakes when they enter the studio!

Caring Isn't A Laughing Matter

When it comes to the issues she feels strongly about, however, Rosie is as serious as they come. In Rosie's words, "I can be very funny and light and that's what the show is mostly. But when I get to something that I'm very serious about, I'm not really entertaining. I become more like a lawyer than a comic." Rosie puts her energy into many different family, health and women's issues. A strong children's advocate, Rosie has adopted four children of her own and in 1997, she established the For All Kids Foundation, which supports charities that help disadvantaged children.

Object Of Desire

"We made a rule – none of the guests are allowed to French kiss the host. It's just the rule! From now on. Richard Simmons tried to do it, Meatloaf. I can't blame them – everyone wants to!"

On Her Mind . . .

"It is sick that I know all these words! Imagine what diseases I could cure if I could empty the useless crap from my brain! It's like a high-speed computer but it only doodles, ya know what I mean?"

Rosie will be making a splash at the newsstands and super-market checkouts as well. She plans to take over the magazine *McCall's*. The new *Rosie's McCall's* will appear in Spring 2001. Rosie fans can look forward to the same kinds of celebrities, honesty, and energy that they have come to adore on the show.

And this past winter, Broadway patrons had the chance to catch Rosie as The Cat in the Hat in the musical, *Seussical*. She says of Broadway, "In 1973, I saw Bette Midler on Broadway and I thought, 'that's what I want to do.'"

In a recent *Today Show* interview with Katie Couric, Rosie implied that she would take her show off the air when her contract expires in 2002. Even though her fans would be disappointed, you can bet the irrepressible Rosie O'Donnell will be heard from – loud and clear!

AP/WWP

Rosie and her friend, Madonna, having some fun with the audience of *The Rosie O'Donnell Show.*

AP/WWP

Regis
Philbin

LIVE With Regis & Kelly

WHO IS REGIS PHILBIN ANYWAY? A veteran of the television industry, Regis is currently at the top of his career as the congenial master of banter on *LIVE With Regis & Kelly* and the host of the hot prime time game show, *Who Wants To Be A Millionaire?*

Birth Name
Regis Francis
Xavier Philbin

Birth Date
August 25, 1933

Birthplace
New York City

Education
B.A., Sociology
University of Notre Dame

Marital Status
Married to Joy Philbin

Children
Amy, Danny,
Joanna, Jennifer (J.J.)

When Regis Philbin's youngest daughter decided to attend Notre Dame, his own alma mater, he was "ecstatic." But "more for me than he was for himself," says J.J. "In a lot of ways, we're alike. We both have a lot of spirit." And that spirit shines through as Regis, after almost 40 years in the business, sits at the top of his career as host of both a wildly popular game show and a favorite morning talk show.

But he remembers how his mother warned him to keep things in perspective. "Whenever she thought I was in danger of getting too big for my britches: 'Hey, Mister Big Shot, the poorhouse is right around the corner!' Mothers have a way of keeping things in perspective. I've never forgotten her words."

The Prediction

In 1970, during the final installment of *The Joey Bishop Show*, guest astrologer Sydney Omarr told Regis, who was then Bishop's sidekick, that his name would become nationally recognized. Regis asked "When is this going to happen?" Omarr replied, "It's going to take 20 years."

Talk To Me!

Regis had always dreamed of becoming a television personality like his idol, Jack Paar, so he began at the bottom of the ladder, as a page at an NBC affiliate in Los Angeles.

This led to jobs as news and sportswriter, and, eventually feature reporter and anchor. Those early shows gave him the opportunity to develop the formula that revolutionized TV talk shows, "host chat." "We had no staff," Regis explains, "No writers, no band. I'd sit on a stool and talk to the audience about whatever I experienced that week, and that's how this dialogue began."

The Slow Climb To The Top

From the early 1960s to the early 1980s, Regis hosted local talk shows across the country. During the time he spent as Joey Bishop's sidekick on *The Joey Bishop Show*, Regis' 11 year marriage to Kay Faylan came to an end. But he went on to discover new love. Working as Joey Bishop's assistant was Regis' future wife, Joy Senese – they married in 1970 and have two daughters, Joanna and J.J. Regis went on to host his own daytime variety show, but his big break came in 1983 when

Mitchel Gerber/Corbis

Regis and his wife, Joy, enjoy a night out.

Career Highlights

TELEVISION:
The Joey Bishop Show
(1967-1970)
LIVE With Regis &
Kathie Lee (1988-2000)
Who Wants To Be A
Millionaire?
(1999-present)
LIVE With Regis
(2000-2001)
LIVE With Regis &
Kelly (2001-present)

FILM:
Little Nicky (2000)
A View from the Top
(2001)

he became a co-host on *The Morning Show* in New York. When Kathie Lee Gifford joined him in 1985, their on-air chemistry pushed the show to the top of the ratings. In 1988, the show was nationally syndicated as *LIVE with Regis & Kathie Lee.*

Throughout the years, viewers have enjoyed the lively banter between Regis and Kathie Lee and the occasional appearances of Regis' wife, Joy, as she filled in for Kathie Lee. There is now a new woman sitting beside Regis every morning on *LIVE*, now that Kathie Lee has given up her co-host chair. Kelly Ripa, a face familiar to soap opera fans, has joined Regis on the show that is now known as *LIVE With Regis & Kelly.*

Regis In Prime Time

Despite Regis' track record, his name didn't jump to anyone's mind when ABC decided to air the British import *Who Wants To Be A Millionaire?* in 1999. "The big names in contention were Phil Donahue, Montel Williams and Maury Povich," Regis recalls. "Regis had to fight for it. Regis had to claw for it. Regis almost had to kill for it." Now no one can imagine anyone but Regis hosting the breakaway hit!

You Gotta Have Heart

Since an angioplasty in 1992, Regis has taken his health and heart condition very seriously. He has become an advocate of healthy eating habits and exercise – he released a workout video in 1993, plays

Who Wants to Dress Like Regis Philbin?

In June 2000, Regis launched his own clothing line, based on those spiffy suits and ties he wears on *Who Wants To Be A Millionaire?* His signature shirts are available in Macy's stores in the U.S. and Canada.

Regis has been honored several times for his accomplishments. He has been nominated 10 times for an EMMY for *LIVE* and *Millionaire*. And he has brought home an EMMY for both *Philbin's People* and *The Regis Philbin Show*.

tennis and has always stressed the importance of a healthy lifestyle.

But his interest goes further than his own personal health – Regis is a spokesperson for the American Heart Association and other children research foundations. His involvement began when his son Danny was born with leg defects which led to amputation. "The Children's Hospital in Los Angeles is the (hospital) that I remember. (Danny) spent almost a year at one stretch. It broke my heart."

Regis Finds the Silver Lining

Although Regis loves to kid about "living under this permanent little dark cloud," he sometimes admits that life isn't that bad. "As I've gotten older," he says. "I'm really enjoying life. I think now more than ever. You know, it's a wonderful world we live in."

Regis and his new co-host, Kelly Ripa, share a laugh on the set of *LIVE with Regis & Kelly*. Kelly replaces Kathie Lee Gifford who left the show in July 2000.

Evan Agostini/Image Direct

Maury
Povich

Maury

WHO IS MAURY POVICH ANYWAY? As host of the show that bears his name, Maury Povich has brought years of TV experience to the afternoon talk show circuit. On his show, his guests come together to resolve their differences, not air their complaints.

Birth Name
Maury Povich

Birth Date
January 17, 1939

Birthplace
Bethesda, Maryland

Resides
New York City

Marital Status
Married to Connie Chung
(news correspondent)

Hobby
Golf

In the ever-changing landscape of television, beloved shows fade from the air and new ones rise to take their place – but Maury Povich is a constant. A veteran of the field with over 30 years of experience, Maury has always been a trendsetter. Now in his fifth decade of being on the air, the silver-haired gent has become a respected figure. And that's quite a change for the reporter who seemed more of a wise guy than a wise man as host of the groundbreaking *A Current Affair*.

Mr. Povich Goes To Washington

Maury's upbringing prepared him for his role as television's marathon man. His father, Shirley, wrote for the *Washington*

But It's Such A Nice Name

When Maury heard that his talk show was going to be called *The Maury Povich Show* he hated the idea and asked Paramount to reconsider. They didn't, and the rest is history!

Post for 75 years! "I definitely use the values I learned from my father," Maury told *The Guardian*. "My sense of fairness, honesty and truthfulness all came from him." Maury, the middle child of three, grew up right in the heart of political jungle – Washington, D.C. – and got his start on the air there at WTTG-TV in 1966.

In 1967, Maury became host of *Panorama*, a midday talk show that blended news and entertainment. Awards and accolades followed, and Maury seemed to be on a fast road to stardom.

Maury married Phyllis Minkoff when he was 23, but found that balancing a blossoming career and a new marriage was a difficult task. Maury, whose jobs took him all over the country, admitted to *PEOPLE* magazine, "I had been consumed by my career and made the tragic error of putting that priority ahead of my family." His marriage to Phyllis ended in divorce, but the couple had two daughters, Amy and Susan

AP/WWP

Maury and his wife, newscaster Connie Chung, together for the camera.

Current Affairs

Career Highlights

TELEVISION:
A Current Affair
(1986-1990)
The Maury Povich Show
(1991-1998)
Twenty One (1999-2000)
Maury (1999-present)

While Maury's personal life was floundering, his career was about to receive a big boost. In 1986, Rupert Murdoch bought the station Maury was working for and picked Maury to anchor a new type of show called *A Current Affair*. This program was the first of many that would give rise to "tabloid" news programs. The subject matter covered on *A Current Affair* ranged from old-fashioned, hard-hitting journalistic exposés to humorous, tongue-in-cheek reports. "We were irreverent and we did the stories no one else would," Maury told *The Indianapolis Star* about his time on *A Current Affair*. "We took our work seriously – but never ourselves."

Maury's five year *"Affair"* ended in 1990. In 1991, *The Maury Povich Show* was launched on daytime television. Just as he had been at the forefront of the tabloid TV phenomenon, Maury now found himself leading the pack of morning talk shows.

A Kinder, Gentler Maury

As host of *The Maury Povich Show*, and later, *Maury*, he has made children and the problems they face in their daily lives the focus of many episodes. "I thought we should bring those kids on, because maybe we'll have a better chance of turning them around if we catch the problem sooner," Maury said to the *New York Daily News*. Maury's success rate with these troubled teens can be seen in the several update episodes that he airs during the season.

Who Wants To Be A Game Show Host?

Maury was under consideration to be the host of *Who Wants To Be A Millionaire*. He turned the job down, but later hosted the game show *Twenty One* in 1999.

It's not surprising that Maury is deeply devoted to children. In 1984, Maury married news anchor Connie Chung and in 1995 after unsuccessful attempts to have a child, the couple adopted their son Matthew. Matthew was just thing to keep the doting dad on his toes.

What does Connie say about life with her husband? "For years I tried to get him to be neater," she once told *PEOPLE* in 1989, "because I'd have to follow him around, picking up behind him." And just like everyone else, Maury likes to relax at the end of the day. Connie explains, "After dinner, Maury is a bed potato. He lies there with his books and television clicker."

Positively Povich

Maury has also put a stake in naysayers who thought his programs would never last. With 30 years under his belt and a popular show currently airing, Maury seems to be destined to continue making waves and setting trends that leave the rest of the television world scrambling to keep pace.

Maury joins his show's audience.

Studios USA

Sally Jesse
Raphael

The Sally Show

WHO IS SALLY JESSE RAPHAEL ANYWAY? She's the daytime talk show hostess and advice guru who is always ready to send troubled teens off to boot camp, give tough-love to her dysfunctional guests or hand them a tissue when emotions run high.

Birth Name
Sally Lowenthal

Birth Date
February 25, 1943

Birthplace
Easton, Pennsylvania

Resides
Pawling, New York,
Manhattan and Nice,
France

Marital Status
Married to Karl Soderlund
(manager for Sally)

Signature Accessory
red-framed glasses

Hobby
Interior Decorating

S ally Jessy Raphael is not simply the woman in red glasses who helps people put their families back together, and their lives on track. She's a wife, a mother and a determined woman who wants only to help people who can benefit from her life experience.

On The Road Again

Sally has never stayed in one place for long. She moved with her parents to New York and then to San Juan, Puerto Rico. Sally lived there for years and still considers the island her home. She hosted her first radio show in San Juan and held a variety of broadcasting jobs there before she landed on television. She attributes her culinary skills to her stint as a cooking show host in South America.

"What Do You Think About . . ."

Sally's reputation for infallible advice follows her everywhere. She says, "If I am in a strange city standing on a street corner, I'm the one people ask for directions. If I'm in a restaurant ladies room, the woman next to me automatically tells me the story of her life!" It must be the glasses, Sally.

Sally also put in some time as a theater and arts critic in various radio stations across the country. Working in Pittsburgh, New York, Miami and New Haven, Connecticut, she sometimes did three air shifts at different stations every day. And it wasn't always smooth going. Sally was fired 18 times and worked in 24 different cities before she took a job at NBC's *Talknet* where she gave advice over the radio from 1981 to 1987. In doing this, she discovered that she enjoyed listening to people's love stories and tragedies. Her success led to a half-hour television advice show in St. Louis which began in 1983.

Sally found success because, according to her, "in those days, there just weren't strong, opinionated women talking about controversial issues on television." Her show was soon syndicated and blossomed into the nationally-recognized *The Sally Show*.

AP/WWP

Sally and her husband, Karl Soderlund, have been together since her early days in radio.

From Daytime To Primetime

Sally describes her show as one that focuses on creating healthy relationships and being a "modern day morality play which often serves as a wake-up call for guests who are on the wrong track." Over the years, she has branched out from her daytime show and starred in and produced movies that do the same.

In 1996, Sally starred as a judge in the television movie *No One Would Tell,* the story of a high school jock who abuses his girlfriend. In this movie, Sally essentially played herself – a calm mediator in the midst of emotional conflict.

For her next project, Sally took on the role of executive producer for the USA true-crime movie, *The Stalking of Laurie Show.* In 1991, Laurie Show was brutally murdered by her high school classmates in an act of jealous rage. Since 1993, when Laurie's mother Hazel was a guest on Sally's show, the young girl's legacy has been close to Sally's heart.

Advice From The Heart

One of the reasons that Sally is so good at giving advice may be because she has suffered through hardships of her own. She raised children from both her first and second marriage, in addition to children she adopted and other children she opened her home to who were in need of a loving family support system.

Her family has endured, in spite of tragedies such as the accidental overdose of over-the-counter medications which claimed the life of her eldest daughter, Alison, in 1992.

And, barely three weeks after Alison's death, Sally's adopted son J.J. was involved in a near-fatal car

Sally, The Artist

Sally's mother, Dede Lowry, was a recognized painter whose work hangs in museums around the country. Sally has her own studio in New York and says she's "an artist experimenting, in search of a style. So far, I favor a big bold look – colorful and splashy."

accident that landed him in a coma. After emerging from his coma, it took a lot of physical therapy to put him back together and he still exhibited signs of traumatic brain injury.

But through it all, Sally has maintained a private tough-as-nails inner strength. Have her family's trials and tribulations made her tough, or did she just call on the strength she had all along? "You do make steel through fire," Sally says.

At Home With Sally

In her spare time, Sally enjoys decorating her homes in Pawling, New York, Manhattan and Nice, France. A gracious host in both her public life on television and her private life with her loved ones, Sally welcomes her friends and family into her homes.

For a personal taste of Sally's hospitality, you can spend a weekend at the Isaac Stover House, a small bed-and-breakfast that she operates in Buck's County, Pennsylvania.

Sally and her staff celebrate her 19th season on the air.

Image Direct

Charlie Rose

The Charlie Rose Show

WHO IS CHARLIE ROSE ANYWAY? Involved in a profession filled with lighthearted entertainment, Charlie Rose shines as a serious journalist who is dedicated to in-depth interviews and insightful commentary. No matter who is on his show, viewers can expect to hear hard news in addition to amusing anecdotes.

Birth Name
Charles Peete Rose Jr.

Birth Date
January 5, 1942

Birthplace
Henderson, North Carolina

Resides
New York City

Marital Status
Single

Hobby
Listening to books on tape

What do the members of the band Metallica, actor Edward Norton, author Anne Rice and French president Jacques Chirac have in common? They've all been featured on *The Charlie Rose Show*, a weeknight interview program that is broadcast on over 200 PBS station affiliates.

Since 1991, veteran broadcaster Charlie Rose has been asking questions of famous celebrities, headline makers, newsworthy personalities and political figures, among others – often with humor, but always remaining true to the serious news. As he puts it, "I am a questioner – not an entertainer, politician or a preacher. I provide the American public with a front-row seat of history."

And he also often devotes more time to the interviews than many of his co-host peers. Charlie explains, "I believe that there is a place in the spectrum of television for really good conversation."

On The Right Track

The son of Charles and Margaret Rose, Charlie spent his youth on the road – the railroad, that is. His father owned a store in Henderson, North Carolina right next to the local tracks. A childhood fascination of books, radio and television may have sparked an early interest in the media, which was only enhanced by Charlie's determination to someday be famous. "I have never in my life said, 'I can't do that.' Not about anything," Charlie stated.

School Daze

After four years devoted to basketball in high school, Charlie entered Duke University as a pre-med student. However, a career in medicine wasn't in the cards for him. A summer spent as an intern for North Carolina Senator B. Everett Jordan left the young Charlie a self-described "political junkie," and his fascination with the world of politics led to a decision to concentrate his studies in history. Graduating in 1964, Charlie enrolled at Duke's law school program, but soon realized that

AP/WWP

Charlie Rose gets down to business with Hillary Rodham Clinton during her 2000 Senate race.

Career Highlights

law was not for him either. "I was in some firm watching a lawyer advise a client one day, and it dawned on me that I was much more interested in the client than the lawyer." Charlie received his law degree in 1968, but his fascination with people in general would stay with him, and serve Charlie well in the years to come.

The Public Sector

When a job at Banker's Trust in New York City proved tedious, Charlie set his sights on journalism. In 1972, he was able to find work as a weekend reporter for New York's WPIX-TV. He finally got his foot in the door, but Charlie had something special in mind – he really wanted to interview the venerable Bill Moyers, host of *Bill Moyers' International Report* on PBS. In 1974, harlie finally got his chance.

Impressed with the young journalist-to-be, Moyers hired Charlie to be the managing editor for his PBS series. Charlie found himself the executive producer of *Bill Moyers' Journal* a year later. At the time, Charlie had no interest in appearing on camera but he eventually became a correspondent for *U.S.A.: People and Politics*. A 1976 interview with Jimmy Carter earned Charlie his first Peabody Award, an award which recognizes achievement and service in the television and radio industry.

Learning The Ropes

When Bill Moyers left public broadcasting in 1976, Charlie, his young protégé began working for NBC, and later co-hosted a Chicago morning show in 1978. After landing a job as program manager for KXAS-TV in Dallas, Texas, he had his work cut out for him. "(A)ll the responsibility was on me," he said. "I was

No Time To Sleep

All throughout his career, Charlie has been known as a die-hard workaholic. During his time in Dallas, it was not uncommon for him to finish up a day at work and then show up again barely six hours later to tape his show!

working alone; I wasn't co-hosting. I produced the show, found the guests, researched the show. It was an extraordinary time for me." Extraordinary enough, it turned out, to warrant a move of *The Charlie Rose Show* to Washington, D.C. in 1981.

In late 1983, CBS hired him to work on *Nightwatch*. It was there that Charlie sharpened his interviewing skills and gained a new following. His 1987 three-hour interview with Charles Manson won Charlie his first Emmy Award. But a term as anchor of FOX's *Personalities* in 1990 left him missing the more serious interview shows he'd done in the past.

Casually Credible

Finally, in 1991, *The Charlie Rose Show* made its debut on PBS. Syndicated nationally two years later, Charlie finally got to show off his interviewing skills. He's proven himself to be a mas-

ter of the casual interview, with the ability to making guests feel at ease on the show. Fashion mogul Donna Karan, by her own admission, had actually forgotten she was on TV when Charlie talked to her. A wide diversity of guests certainly hasn't hurt Charlie's credibility either. Nearly everyone with a dose of fame has turned up at Charlie's table.

Who else can make a viewer feel perfectly at home and get them thinking at the same time?

Charlie and friend at a
New York City movie premiere.

Reuers NewMedia/Corbis

Dr. Laura
Schlessinger

*The Dr. Laura
Schlessinger Program*

WHO IS DR. LAURA ANYWAY? If you like your advice tough, honest but with a dose of compassion, then you should call Dr. Laura! Television and radio talk show host Dr. Laura has been helping and entertaining people for over a decade with her no-nonsense attitude regarding society's problems.

Birth Name
Laura C. Schlessinger

Birth Date
January 16, 1947

Birthplace
Brooklyn, New York

Education
B.S., Biological Sciences
State University of New
York, Stonybrook
M.S., Ph. D., Physiology
Columbia University

Marital Status
Married to
Dr. Lewis G. Bishop
(neurophysiologist)

Children
Deryk

When you take a glimpse at Dr. Laura's life, you wonder how she has gotten away with saying the things she does – especially over the airwaves! "You can't use my career as a blueprint," she once said, "because this is bizarre. My life is bizarre."

A Lifetime Ago

Details of her early life are sketchy, but Laura does admit that her childhood was not a happy one. After obtaining her B.S. in biological sciences at SUNY in Stonybrook, she went on to earn several advanced degrees in physiology from Columbia University, including her Ph.D. (thus the title "Dr."). She married young and, after a brief marriage, Laura separated from her first husband.

> ## Dr. Laura On Her Work
>
> "My preaching, teaching and nagging all boils down to setting priorities. This is an era that, sadly, focuses on self-actualization, self-satisfaction and basic selfishness. Well, I'm gonna tell you the best mode of selfishness – doing what will ultimately give you a profound sense of gratification."

She moved to California, where the doors to the talk show world opened for her – as a guest! She called Los Angeles talk show personality Bill Ballance in response to his question "Would you rather be a widow or a divorcee?" (Her answer: "a widow, because then everyone feels badly for you.")

Laura impressed Ballance with her wit and enthusiasm, and the two eventually had a brief relationship and she had a brief turn at hosting a radio show, at Bill's side. Their relationship didn't last but, as we'll see later, Bill wasn't out of her life completely!

The Family's The Thing

Laura met her current husband, Lew Bishop, while she was earning her counseling certification at USC. The world changed for her when she and Lew had their son, Deryk, in 1986. Formerly career-oriented, Laura now became the textbook mother. She

stopped working and stayed home to raise her son. But within a few years, after her husband suffered a heart attack, she returned to radio to help support the family.

And she returned to the scene with a bang! Gone was the career-minded feminist that everyone knew, and in her place was the tough-talking, family-oriented

Dr. Laura on the public speaking circuit.

Career Highlights

BOOKS

Ten Stupid Things
Women Do To Mess Up
Their Lives (1994)

Ten Stupid Things Men
Do To Mess Up Their
Lives (1997)

The Ten Commandments:
The Significance of God's
Laws In Everyday Life
(1998)

Parenthood By Proxy:
Don't Have Them If You
Won't Raise Them (2000)

and religion-friendly talk show host who wanted to give an ailing society a dose of "traditional" morality. Laura's values hit a nerve with callers and by 1994, her show went into syndication.

Spreading The Word

The *Dr. Laura Schlessinger Program* reaches millions of listeners every night. Her focus is on moral issues and her callers present problems that deal with topics including premarital sex and sibling rivalry. But don't be fooled – even if you are her biggest fan, Dr. Laura is going to tell you what you need to hear, not necessarily what you want to hear! She's quick with a one-liner and cuts right to the heart of the matter.

Her hard-line stance on several controversial issues has certainly garnered criticism – especially for her outspoken opposition to homosexuality. Laura has also been labeled a "hypocrite" for promoting traditional values even though she's been divorced. And some people speculate that she may have been involved with Lew while he was married to someone else. Her response to these charges is vintage Laura: "A hypocrite is someone who says, 'Do as I say, not as I do.' A teacher is someone who says, 'Do as I do, not as I did.'"

Laura faced probably her biggest emotional challenge in 1998, when ex-lover Bill Ballance was paid $50,000 from an Internet group in exchange for nude photos he took of her when they were together. Though her lawsuit to have the photos removed from the

Too Much Of A Good Thing

When Dr. Laura launched her web site (*www.drlaura.com*), over 300,000 fans hit it the first day – and crashed it!

Internet failed, Laura has dealt with this issue with classic honesty and pragmatism: "In my 20s, I was my own moral authority," she said. "The inadequacy of that way of life is painfully obvious today."

Charity and Children

Much of Laura's charitable work goes toward helping children in need. In 1998, she launched The Dr. Laura Foundation, which oversees the "My Stuff" program which helps spread warmth and comfort to children rescued from abusive homes. Kids are given their own special bag of goodies, such as toiletries, teddy bears and their very own "blankie." Over 10,000 "My Stuff" bags have been distributed to date.

Dr. Laura In Your Home

To the delight of her fans, Dr. Laura launched a daily TV show in the fall of 2000. As on her radio show, Laura tackles issues ranging from cheating spouses to homosexuality and abortion. She also reaches people through *Perspective*, her monthly magazine. And, if that weren't enough, you can also enjoy Hasbro's "Dr. Laura Game," where you and up to 6 players can hash out moral conundrums based on real calls to Dr. Laura's radio show!

Audience members and staff prepare for the next taping of *The Dr. Laura Schlessinger Program.*

AP/WWP

Jerry Springer

The Jerry Springer Show

WHO IS JERRY SPRINGER ANYWAY? This former public servant and mayor of Cincinnati now serves the public in a different capacity as host – some would say ringmaster – of the wildly over-the-top *The Jerry Springer Show*.

Birth Name
Gerald Norman Springer

Birth Date
February 13, 1944

Birthplace
London, England

Marital Status
Single

Notable Act
Had a very active role in lowering the voting age to 18 during the 1960s

B olt down your chairs, cover your children's eyes and strap yourself in for the wildest hour on morning television. Prudish critics, toned-down fights and rumors of fixed shows couldn't stop Jerry Springer's rise to the top. In fact, with a divorce from Micki Velton and a few personal scandals under his belt, perhaps he would even make a very good guest on one of his shows.

The People's Politician

With a B.A. in political science from Tulane University (1965) and a law degree from Northwestern University (1968), Jerry became a political wonder boy who got his start campaigning for Senator Robert F. Kennedy's 1968 presidential bid. Then in 1971, Jerry was elected to his first of five consecutive terms as Cincinnati councilman, although he resigned from office in 1977 after it was revealed that he paid for a prostitute with a personal check. Bouncing back, Jerry was elected mayor in 1977 – one of the country's youngest ever (at age 33) – after he earned the largest plurality of votes.

After his amazingly popular stint as mayor, Jerry didn't miss a beat when he moved effortlessly into the newsroom, where he anchored the news on WLWT-TV. In addition to the seven Emmy Awards he added to his mantel, he also garnered Best Anchor honors five years in a row from the readers of *Cincinnati Magazine*.

Although Jerry was initially against the idea, management at the station believed he was popular enough to host his very own talk show. On September 30, 1991, *The Jerry Springer Show* was born and, after the the show was tweaked to include strippers, brawlers and cheating spouses, the ratings began to climb. Chants of "Jer-ry! Jer-ry!" rang loudly through the studio audiences as they

Jerry reacts to a fan during an entertainment convention autographing session.

Career Highlights

TELEVISION:
The Jerry Springer Show
(1991-present)

FILM:
Ringmaster (1998)

witnessed such topics as "I Married A Horse" and "Honey, I'm A Prostitute." And how do they come up with such titles? Well, according to Jerry, "We go out drinking."

Jerry Versus His Critics

What do the critics think of such entertainment? "King of Sleaze" and "Sultan of Slime" are just some of the many comments hurled Jerry's way. What is the host's take on the whole thing? "It's not the subjects that amaze me – it's the fact that people are willing to share their secrets." An interesting comment coming from a man who seems to be followed around by scandals and allegations of keeping company with people of "questionable" moral status.

Jerry would admit, "Our show is the stupidest on television" He even states, "There's no reason a shlub like me should be a success. A dolt could do what I do." But his millions of fans would disagree and it's difficult to argue the show's role as a First Amendment trailblazer.

Jerry's belief in First Amendment rights has deep roots. Jerry was born in London in 1944 and lost many family members to the Holocaust before fleeing to America, where he remembers passing through Ellis Island and seeing the Statue of Liberty when he was 5 years old. He has said, "America survives because we permit all ideas to be aired, then common sense and logic win out." And also, "Just because you interview people, or permit them to be before the camera does not mean that you endorse them. Otherwise every anchor in America would be in jail."

On The Air And In The News

Jerry has used his broad appeal to branch out into other mediums. He described his first feature film, the 1998 movie *Ringmaster*, with

Call Him Dr. Talk

To promote the release of his country music album *Dr. Talk*, Jerry toured with singer Billy Ray Cyrus.

Groovy, Baby

Jerry played himself in the 1999 comedy *Austin Powers: The Spy Who Shagged Me.* In an example of art mirroring life, the film featured a segment of Jerry's show in which Dr. Evil and his son air their strife (and, of course, a fight breaks out between the guests!).

his usual honesty by saying "Siskel and Ebert are going to wish they had a third thumb so they could stick it right up my a--." Jerry's first book, also titled *Ringmaster*, offered readers a personal perspective on Jerry's life and show.

Citizen Jerry

Jerry has hosted *The Jerry Lewis Labor Day Telethon* and has served as vice president for the national Muscular Dystrophy Association. His only child, Katie, was born legally blind, deaf in one ear and with a multitude of other physical disabilities and this may be the reason for Jerry's involvement in several children's charities and fund-raising efforts for medical research.

You can love him or you can hate him, but it is impossible to ignore him. As long as Jerry keeps making headlines on and off the air, *The Jerry Springer Show* will continue to be the first choice for daytime viewers who crave on-air excitement and escapades.

Always the entertainer, Jerry talks to fans during an event at Planet Hollywood in New York.

Everett Collection

Meredith
Vieira

The View

WHO IS MEREDITH VIEIRA ANYWAY? Meredith Vieira is one of the most colorful personalities on *The View*. Her years of experience in the television news industry make her one of the most respected personalities in TV, and make her own show just that much more professional.

Birth Name
Meredith Vieira

Birth Date
December 30, 1953

Birthplace
Providence, Rhode Island

Resides
Westchester County,
New York

Marital Status
Married to Richard Cohen
(television producer)

Children
Ben, Gabe, Lily

M eredith Vieira's background in broadcast journalism didn't exactly prepare her for giving lap dances to Wesley Snipes or wearing fake breasts, just two of her many on-air stunts on *The View*, but there are many facets to this Emmy Award-winning news journalist and two-time recipient of *PEOPLE*'s "50 Most Beautiful People In The World" honor.

Rise To The Top

Raised in Providence, Rhode Island, Meredith attended college at Tufts University in Massachusetts. Her first news assignments came at radio station WORC in Worcester. After that, she worked in Providence before eventually landing in New York City at WCBS-TV.

Here She Is . . .

In 1998, Meredith hosted the Miss America Pageant with former football quarterback Boomer Esiason. Regarding the famous swimsuit competition, Meredith quipped, "I don't think Boomer should be in a two-piece."

This prepared her for a job at CBS News, where she reported from the network's Chicago bureau. Meredith rose quickly within the ranks of CBS. First, with *West 57th*, and later for the *CBS Evening News With Dan Rather*, she established herself as one of the network's top correspondents.

This led to her being offered the crown jewel in CBS's broadcasting crown – a job as correspondent on *60 Minutes*. Only 36 years old at the time, Meredith joined such veterans as Mike Wallace and Morley Safer.

A Different View . . .

Unlike the famous ticking stopwatch that begins every episode of the show, things did not run smoothly for Meredith on the set of *60 Minutes*. When she requested time off to have her second child, this was not well received and Meredith felt as if she was being attacked in the media. "For a while they were criticizing my work in the press and I thought it was unfair. They sort of stabbed at my professional integrity and I thought that was wrong," the star once explained.

Meredith (front center) is shown with her *View* co-hosts, including Debbie Matenopoulos who was later replaced by Lisa Ling.

A Change In View

Meredith found a change of scenery at ABC, where she became chief correspondent for the news show *Turning Point,* which aired for 4 years.

When Meredith's contract was up with *Turning Point* in 1997, Barbara Walters offered her a seat on the brand new morning talk and variety program Barbara was developing for ABC. Although it took some time to find its niche, *The View* became one of daytime television's runaway success stories among women viewers of all ages.

Coming Into Her Own

Meredith blossomed in her new forum, winning over viewers with her warmth, skill and charisma, although her natural spontaneity has sometimes landed Meredith in the hot seat. Eyebrows were raised when Meredith asked baseball player Mike Piazza which player had the "biggest wood" on the Mets. Responding to the Piazza fracas, Meredith denied she was at the game as a journalist, saying, "I was there having fun." But most viewers have responded positively to the previously unknown fun side of Meredith Vieira.

And Meredith has found that new side of hers liberating. "For 20 years, I wasn't a commentator, but an objective reporter," she told the *Buffalo News* in 1998. "Being asked to be myself and inject my own opinions feels good . . . (i)t's nice to be seen as a person rather than a career."

All Shook Up

Meredith caused quite a stir when she revealed to Kenneth Brannagh on *The View* that she once married an Elvis impersonator in Las Vegas, only to have the marriage annulled because he wasn't really The King. Although she was only joking, the story was picked up by *TV Guide*, *USA Today* and *Star*.

Wife And Mother First, Reporter Second

Meredith's on-camera smiles have often hidden some personal tears. Her husband Richard, after successfully beating colon cancer, has had to face the oncoming symptoms of multiple sclerosis. Meredith has been strong for her husband and family during this difficult period, telling *Ladies Home Journal*, "Richard does not pity himself, so it's not fair for me to." She's always found both strength and escape in her family, and an interview with *The Westchester WAG* details her house as a lovingly cluttered home, perfect for raising her close-knit family.

What does the future hold for Meredith? As her three children get older, Meredith is beginning to consider a career in children's television. "I see what my own kids watch and what I'd like them to be watching, so some day, I may be doing something to enhance that medium," she said in a *New York Times* interview. Fans of this multitalented wife, mother and moderator can look forward to seeing Meredith branch out into other areas of the television industry – and give us still another view of the world.

Andrew Eccles/ABC

Meredith (third from left) and her early *The View* co-hosts relax for a photo opportunity.

AP/WWP

Barbara
Walters

The View

WHO IS BARBARA WALTERS ANYWAY? Barbara's hard-hitting news reporting, her ground-breaking celebrity interviews and her memorable personality have propelled her through the tough world of television news to become a broadcasting legend and a host of her own show.

Birth Name
Barbara Walters

Birth Date
September 25, 1931

Birthplace
Boston, Massachusetts

Resides
New York City

Marital Status
Single

Famous Friend
Beverly Sills
(opera singer)

When veteran news correspondent Barbara Walters first brought the idea for *The View* to ABC, it was not well received. Who would want to watch five women, all from different backgrounds and generations, chatting over coffee? But Barbara knew better!

The View has been amusing and informing viewers since its debut in 1997. For Barbara – the show's creator, co-owner, co-producer and occasional host – it's been a long trip to become the "first lady" of television news. According to former ABC News head, Roone Arledge, "She just keeps getting better and better. She has a way of getting people to say things on the air that they never thought they were going to say."

> ### Someone's In The Kitchen With Barbara
>
> After being verbally grilled for six hours, Cuban leader, Fidel Castro, did some grilling of his own. He made everyone grilled cheese sandwiches, about which Barbara is quoted as saying, ". . . they weren't bad."

"Today Girl" To Million-Dollar Anchor

Perhaps Barbara feels so comfortable around celebrities today because she was surrounded by them during her youth. Lou Walters, her father, was the founder and owner of the tremendously popular Latin Quarter nightclubs in New York which were frequented by celebrities like Milton Berle and Frank Sinatra.

Barbara attended three different high schools in only four years, but her mom Dena, a housewife, kept Barbara's home life stable. Barbara once told an interviewer that she remembers being "a kid who was angry and skinny and introverted." But, in 1953, her father faced bankruptcy. He also had a heart attack and the days of the glitz and glamour were over. Barbara had to go to work to support her parents and her mentally handicapped older sister, Jacqueline. She began to work in television, producing and writing for local New York stations like WNBC-TV.

Barbara was eventually hired in 1961 as

Barbara shows off her Lifetime Achievement Award during the 2000 Daytime Emmy Award Show.

Career Highlights

TELEVISION:
Today (1961-1976)
Not For Women Only
(1972-1976)
ABC Evening News
(1976-1978)
20/20 (1979-present)
The View (1997-present)

the sole female writer for NBC's morning show *Today*, and has said, "I was only allowed to write 'female things.' I could do fashion shows. I could do celebrity interviews." She remained with the show for another 10 years until she was promoted to full co-host in 1974.

Show Me The Money!

During her time on *Today*, Barbara refined her interviewing style and journalistic skills. Her success led to a co-anchor position with Harry Reasoner on *ABC's Evening News* in 1976. She was the first woman to anchor a network evening newscast and was given a five-year contract for $1 million a year. The first of Barbara's interview specials also debuted in 1976. Other firsts soon followed, including a joint interview in 1977 with Egyptian President Anwar Sadat and Israeli Prime Minister Menachem Begin and a lengthy interview with Cuba's Fidel Castro. In 1979, ABC shifted Barbara to *20/20* where she became a co-anchor with Hugh Downes in 1984, where you can still see her on Friday nights.

I Get No Respect

Succeeding in a male-dominated field like broadcasting was no easy feat for Barbara, especially when she made a point of interviewing Hollywood celebrities as well as world political figures. She also had to defend herself against critics who thought she was being paid too much. Barbara disagreed strongly, saying that "Mike Douglas was making something like $10 million . . . and nobody criticized him."

Barbara's Boys

Barbara has dated her share of famous men. In her younger days, she dated Roy Cohn, aide to Senator Joseph McCarthy. Her more recent paramours have included Senator John Warner, Elizabeth Taylor's ex-husband and – or so it was rumored – Alan Greenspan!

Saturday Night Barbara

Barbara's unique voice has lent itself to comedy: *Saturday Night Live's* Gilda Radner (who referred to Barbara as "Baba Wawa") and Cheri Oteri have parodied her.

Humble Pie

Offscreen, Barbara is still the warm, friendly person we see on TV but, by her own admission, she is on the shy side. "People think I have all the guts in the world," she has said, "but it's hard for me to pick up the phone." Instead of hobnobbing with celebrities, Barbara likes to spend time with her friends, many of whom she has known since college. She also enjoys spending time with her daughter, Jacqueline. And Barbara's favorite spot to relax is in the bathtub! How does Barbara see herself? Indecisive: "When I die, it's going to say on my tombstone, 'On the other hand, maybe I should have lived.'"

While she may claim to be an ordinary person, it is really impossible to overlook Barbara's immense achievements. She has won many prestigious awards, including both Daytime and Primetime Emmy Awards, and has also been honored with an impressive five honorary doctorates!

Barbara has interviewed every president from Nixon to Clinton. But most importantly, she paved the way for women broadcasters, like Jane Pauley and Diane Sawyer, who would follow in her footsteps.

Evan Agostini/Image Direct

Barbara strikes a pose at the 2000 opening of an art exhibit in New York City.

The Everett Collection

Montel
Williams

The Montel Williams Show

WHO IS MONTEL WILLIAMS ANYWAY? Loyal fans know that when Montel Williams speaks, he speaks from the heart. Known for tackling hard issues with integrity and respect, Montel brings his energy and sense of commitment to millions of viewers every day.

Birth Name
Montel Brian Williams

Birth Date
July 3, 1956

Birthplace
Baltimore, Maryland

Marital Status
Single

Children
Ashley, Maressa,
Montel II, Wyntergrace

Favorite Watchwords
"Restraint, Responsibility,
Respect"

In the fun and flighty world of daytime talk shows, Montel stands out. Not only is he one of the most dedicated and respected hosts in the business, but he is also a gifted actor, writer and motivational speaker. Whether he's dealing with other people's challenges or his own, Montel has a knack for turning adversity into advantage.

Early Years

As one of four children raised in urban Baltimore in the 1950s, Montel has seen many of life's difficulties first-hand. His parents were both hard workers. Montel reflects, "This was in the 1950s in America. Black people got paid one thing, white people got paid another."

Montel On Respect And Communication

"One of the most glaring problems I've noticed, after talking to thousands of families across the country, is that people just don't know how to talk to each other anymore."

After graduating from high school in 1974, Montel enlisted in the United States Marine Corps. He went on to Navy Prep School and later the United States Naval Academy in Annapolis, Maryland, where he studied engineering and international security. He became an intelligence officer after graduation, served aboard several vessels through the 1980s and was recognized with many awards and honors.

Career Change

As a successful military officer, Montel had great motivational skills. In 1988, he started counseling servicemen and their families on all sorts of issues. When he went to a Kansas City, Missouri, high school to talk to students about leadership and determination, Montel knew he had a new career on his hands. He renounced his commission and devoted himself to motivational speaking.

In 1991, Montel established his own talk show, in which he could have his very own public forum to help many people through the power of television. And so *The Montel Williams Show* was born.

Montel – at home in front of the microphone.

Career Highlights

TELEVISION:
The Montel Williams
Show (1991-present)
A Different World (1992)
Matt Waters (1996)
The New Adventures of
Robin Hood (1997)
JAG
(1997, 1999)

FILM:
The Peacekeeper (1997)
Little Pieces, director
(2000)

Montel On The Air

Montel's main goal is to focus on important problems and work to find solutions. Forget the strippers and public fights. He tackles all sorts of everyday issues, among them, alcoholism, illiteracy and family relations, and sometimes explores less traditional topics like psychic ability and metaphysical events.

A big part of his mission is the show's "After-Care" program. In 1992, Montel hired a psychologist to work with guests to find the right counseling and services to help them deal with their problems once the cameras stopped rolling.

Hundreds of guests have been helped by Montel's "After-Care" program, and you can tell that he is very proud of it (as he should be). "Just like the cliché says, 'Talk is cheap,'" Montel says. "Unless we do something about these problems – go beyond talking and start taking action – nothing will change. Our show is committed to helping people develop solutions by rolling up our sleeves and getting involved."

Personal Challenges

And maybe one of the reasons that he feels so strongly about this mission is the amount of adversity he's had to deal with in his very own life. In 1999, Montel was shocked to learn that he was suffering from multiple sclerosis (MS), a degenerative disease in which the body's white blood cells attacks its own nerves.

Communication

For more information about multiple sclerosis or The Montel Williams MS Foundation, contact the foundation at:

The Montel Williams
MS Foundation
331 W. 57th Street
New York, NY 10019
(212) 830-0347

Grace-ful Exit

Soon after Montel disclosed his illness, he stunned his friends and fans by revealing that he and his second wife, Grace, were divorcing after seven years of marriage. Montel called the divorce "the hardest thing I've had to deal with next to MS."

To help fight the disease, Montel has established The Montel Williams MS Foundation. "MS picked the wrong person," he once said in signature Montel style. "I have a big mouth and I am going to continue flapping it until there is a cure!" In 2000, Montel announced his Cure for Multiple Sclerosis Poetry Contest in conjunction with the International Library of Poetry (*www.poetry.com*).

The Mission Continues

Despite these personal challenges, Montel has kept his positive outlook and sense of commitment to others. As a follow-up to his 1996 autobiography, *Mountain, Get Out Of My Way*, Montel published *Life Lessons and Reflections in 2000*, which is a collection of photographs and inspirational words. This book was written by Montel to offer comfort and personal motivation, with proceeds from the sales supporting his multiple sclerosis foundation. It is all a part of his mission to help people to help themselves through a course of inspiration and action.

Montel questions a guest at a taping of his show,
The Montel Williams Show.

Nick Elgar/Image Direct

Oprah
Winfrey

The Oprah Winfrey Show

WHO IS OPRAH WINFREY ANYWAY? She's the undisputed queen of daytime television, a talented actress and producer, a literacy advocate and one of the most respected voices in entertainment.

Birth Name
Oprah Gail Winfrey

Birth Date
January 29, 1954

Birthplace
Kosciusko, Mississippi

Resides
Chicago

Marital Status
Single

Famous Friend
Toni Morrison
(author)

Few people in show business can match Oprah Winfrey's winning combination of drive, intelligence and sensitivity. In many ways, Oprah's dramatic life story reads like one of the books in her club or a rags-to-riches Hollywood drama.

A Rough Beginning

Oprah was born in rural Mississippi to two unwed teenagers. She was first named "Orpah," after a figure from the Bible, but a misspelling on her birth certificate produced the name "Oprah."

One of her earliest positive influences was her grandmother, a religious woman who raised Oprah on her farm. She brought Oprah to church with her, where the youngster quickly developed a reputation as a good reader and a vocal child. Oprah explained in an interview, "I used to speak in the church all the time, and the sisters in the front row would say to my grandmother, 'Hattie Mae, this child sure can talk.'"

Oprah stayed with her grandmother until she was 6, then went to live with her mother in Milwaukee, Wisconsin. Her years there turned out to be a disaster. She was sexually abused by a cousin and uncle, she abused drugs and alcohol and, when she was only 14, gave birth to a premature baby who died soon afterwards.

Begins To Turn Around

But Oprah persevered through these early adversities. She moved to Nashville, Tennessee to live with her father and, under his discipline and support, began to turn her life around. His high standards and encouragement helped her improve in school and raise her self confidence. Oprah wanted to be an actress from the time she was a little girl, but her father took a dim view of it. So she took another media path – journalism.

Oprah and her boyfriend, Stedman Graham, enjoy a night out on the town.

Career Highlights

TELEVISION:
The Oprah Winfrey
Show (1986-present)
The Women of Brewster
Place (1989)
The Fresh Prince
of Bel-Air (1992)
Ellen (1997)
FILM:
The Color Purple (1985)
Native Son (1986)
Throw Momma
From the Train (1987)
Beloved (1998)

Finding Her Niche

Oprah found her true calling when she took a job as news anchor at WTVF in Nashville – becoming the station's youngest (and first female African-American) anchor.

Her first talk-show hosting gig came at a Baltimore television station, on a show called *People Are Talking*. This was a much better fit for Oprah, who said in an interview that she "did not do so well as a news reporter," because she empathized too much while interviewing victims of tragedy.

Then, it was on to Chicago, where, in 1984, Oprah took on the then-king of daytime talk, Phil Donahue. Her half-hour show, *A.M. Chicago,* was opposite Donahue's time slot and tested Oprah's skills early. Within a year, she was the talk of the town and expanded her show to a full hour. In 1986, *The Oprah Winfrey Show* found a national audience with a syndication deal – and a legend was born!

Empathy Is Key

Now, 15 years later, Oprah has fended off stiff challenges by the likes of Jerry Springer and Rosie O'Donnell to keep her position as the #1 talk show on television. Twenty-two million people tune in to Oprah each day, and her show is broadcast to over 100 countries worldwide.

What makes Oprah so popular? If there is one reason, it's honesty. Oprah engages her audience on an intimate level, reassures them that everyone has dreams, problems and stories to tell. When Oprah offers a hug to a grieving guest, or sheds tears of joy over a guest's successful battle

Time Will Tell

"You can have it all. You just can't have it all at one time."

Let Oprah Fill Up Your Bookshelf

Oprah's Book Club, launched in 1996, is Oprah's way to encourage people to read. After reading potential book club selections (and yes, she does read them first!), Oprah selects her favorite and then hosts a televised book discussion with her viewers. Is it just a coincidence that most of her selections go on to become best sellers?

with cancer, this is a show of how she genuinely feels.

More Than Just Talk

But the multi-talented Oprah isn't "just" a talk show host. In 1985, she realized her childhood dream and made her acting debut in Steven Spielberg's film *The Color Purple*.

Oprah's generosity has also benefited many different charities over the years. In 1997, she she launched Oprah's Angel Network, which encourages people to donate to various worthy causes like scholarships and Habitat for Humanity.

More than any other talk show host, Oprah has shown just how much an entertainer can affect the lives of millions of "ordinary" people every day. Maybe that's the real reason she's the class of the talk-show crowd!

Pop star Michael Jackson shows Oprah the sights at his California ranch before her live interview with him in 1993.

Talk Show Legends

S ome made you laugh, some made you cry and others made you think. Over the years, news and variety talk shows have produced some of television's most memorable personalities.

AP/WWP

Steve
Allen

The Tonight Show, 1954-1957

Allen launched *The Tonight Show* and tickled fans for 40 years with other productions like *The Steve Allen Show* and *The Big Show*.

AP/WWP

William F.
Buckley Jr.

Firing Line, 1966-1999

Buckley's program set the standard for political debate shows, and his conservative viewpoint provoked thought for over 30 years.

AP/WWP

Johnny
Carson

The Tonight Show, 1962-1992

The third host of *The Tonight Show* is one of the most recognizable figures in show business. Carson's humor sent generations to bed with a smile.

AP/WWP

Dick
Cavett

The Dick Cavett Show, 1968-1975, 1977-1982

Cavett is best known for his historic interview with the reclusive John Lennon and Yoko Ono in the 1970s.

Corbis

Phil
Donahue
Donahue, 1967-1996

All issue-oriented talk shows owe much to Donahue. As the first host to actively engage the audience, he was a friendly and intelligent voice on afternoon TV.

AP/WWP

Mike
Douglas
The Mike Douglas Show, 1961-1982

Douglas pioneered the daytime entertainment-talk-variety show. A former singer, Douglas was a true fan of Hollywood who had celebrity guests co-host on a regular basis.

AP/WWP

Kathie Lee
Gifford
LIVE With Regis & Kathie Lee, 1989-2000

She's the poster child for "perky," a diamond in the rough of Hollywood. Loyal Kathie Lee fans can now enjoy following her acting career.

AP/WWP

Virginia
Graham
Girl Talk, 1963-1969

The "first lady" of early afternoon talk shows, Graham set a standard from the 1950s to 1970s with shows like *Food For Thought* and *The Virginia Graham Show*.

AP/WWP

Merv
Griffin

The Merv Griffin Show,
1962-1963, 1965-1986

Media mogul Griffin gained fame as one of the most savvy and influential entertainers around. As a producer, he brought *Jeopardy!* to TV in 1984.

AP/WWP

Charles
Kuralt

CBS News Sunday Morning,
1979-1994

The beloved poet laureate of TV journalism, Kuralt made average America come alive, beginning with *On The Road* (1967-1980).

AP/WWP

John
McLaughlin

The McLaughlin Group, 1982-current

Funny, sarcastic and just a bit cantankerous, this veteran journalist and ex-presidential speechwriter hosts the liveliest public affairs roundtable on television.

AP/WWP

Ed
McMahon

The Tonight Show, 1962-1992

McMahon has proved that he's much more than the world's most famous second banana. He not only gave us "Heeeeeere's Johnny!," but he hosted *Star Search* for 12 years.

Edward R.
Murrow
Person To Person, 1953-1959

After his World War II radio broad-casts, Murrow made the transition to television. His informal show *Person To Person* sometimes interviewed guests in their own homes.

Jack
Paar
The Tonight Show, 1957-1962

Before there was Johnny, there was Jack. Paar brought a different tone to the show, giving politicians and other public figures camera time alongside entertainers.

Geraldo
Rivera
Geraldo/The Geraldo Rivera Show, 1987-1998

The former *20/20* journalist has cer-tainly had his share of headlines over the years! He currently hosts and co-hosts two shows for CNBC.

Dinah
Shore
The Dinah Shore Show, 1951-1957

The talk show career of this talented singer and actress spanned 30 years, with popular programs like *Dinah's Place* (1970-1974) and *Dinah!* (1974-1980).

Tom
Snyder
Tomorrow, 1973-1982

Cultured, clever and quirky might be the best words to describe Snyder, whose talk show came on the heels of a 40-year journalism career.

Ed
Sullivan
The Ed Sullivan Show, 1948-1971

As the host of the longest-running TV variety show in history, Sullivan introduced the Beatles to America in 1964, and showcased a young comedian named Richard Pryor.

David
Susskind
The David Susskind Show, 1967-1987

Before his PBS run, Susskind hosted *Open End* (1958-1967), a talk show that sometimes lasted for hours! His 1960 interview with Nikita Krushchev made world headlines.

Dr. Ruth
Westheimer
The Dr. Ruth Show, 1984

She didn't invent sex, but you might think she did! The irrepressible psychosexual therapist has been promoting "sexual literacy" through TV and radio shows for 20 years.

Do You Remember . . . ?

Somewhere between the popular hosts of today and the legends of yesterday lie the "also-rans." Some were good, some were not-so-good and others were just plain ugly! See if you remember catching any of these hosts during their time in the talk show sun!

The Good

From 1995 to 1999, veteran actor and current *60 Minutes II* commentator Charles Grodin hosted *The Charles Grodin Show*, on CNBC and later MSNBC. Given his list of "harmless" movie credits and his deadpan demeanor, you'd think his show would have suffered from a "boredom factor." But Grodin turned heads and furrowed brows with his acidic commentary, evil stares and sarcastic smirks as he blasted every issue that came his way. Whatever you may have thought of Grodin's onstage antics, he didn't last five years for nothing!

The same can be said for Arsenio Hall. From 1989 to 1994, *The Arsenio Hall Show* was a legitimate rival to Carson, Letterman and later Leno on the late-night scene. Hall had made "whoo whoo whoo" a household term and, most importantly, found a solid niche by attracting younger viewers who weren't turned on by the late-night TV establishment. Perhaps it was his sax appeal. During the 1992 presidential election, Arsenio introduced Bill Clinton to a new generation of young voters when Clinton

Arsenio Hall strikes a pose in this photo from 1994, the final year his show, *The Arsenio Hall Show*, was aired.

appeared as Arsenio's guest and wowed the crowd by blowing "Heartbreak Hotel" on his saxophone. In many ways, Arsenio was a late-night trendsetter. No other show could boast controversial guests like Louis Farrakhan and Andrew Dice Clay on their rosters!

Sports fans are familiar with longtime sportscaster Bob Costas, who had one of the most successful talk show runs in recent memory. *Later With Bob Costas*, which ran from 1988 to 1994, wasn't so much a classic talk show as a one-on-one interview show. Costas consistently got great reviews and even won an Emmy Award in 1993.

Another Emmy Award-winning talk show host was none other than comedienne, author and self-proclaimed big mouth, Joan Rivers! Rivers cut her talk show teeth as a frequent guest host for Johnny Carson's *Tonight Show* in the 1980s and eventually hosted *The Late Show* from 1986 to 1987. She resurfaced two years later to host a popular syndicated show until 1993. Her famous bread-and-butter was Hollywood gossip, spun in her frantic style while holding her four-legged "co-host," her dog Spike!

AP/WWP

Donny and Marie Osmond, the brother and sister 1970s singing duo, returned to television with their own talk show in 1998.

Daytime talk turned nice in 1998 when brother and sister duo Donny and Marie Osmond returned to the airwaves after a 20-year hiatus. Their loyal fans loved their old-style variety show tone, not to mention their brother-sister chemistry. *Donny & Marie* had a pretty good run before it was cancelled in 2000 for financial reasons.

The Not-So-Good

Outside of these success stories, most talk shows have come and gone quickly – mostly for one simple reason: bad ratings.

Carnie Wilson has made recent headlines for her gastric bypass operation, which resulted in her losing nearly half her body weight. But the former Wilson Phillips band member and daughter of founding Beach Boy Brian Wilson also had her own daytime talk show in 1995. According to legend, she got *Carnie* after a TV executive heard her go head-to-head with Howard Stern and thought she'd be a talk show natural. But she never drew an audience and *Carnie* folded after only one season.

Comic Howie Mandel hosted his own show between 1998 and 1999. Howie certainly had comedic talent and a loyal core of fans, but he just never caught on with viewers. Ditto for Martin Short, whose talk/variety show lasted only one season.

One of the biggest names to take a stab at a talk show was mega-superstar Whoopi

APWWP

Comedian Howie Mandel also attempted talk show hosting during the late 1990s.

Goldberg, who opted for the one-on-one interview format with *The Whoopi Goldberg Show* in 1992. Hers was a unique talk show, more friendly than feisty, during its year on the air.

As the longtime host of *Wheel of Fortune*, Pat Sajak became an unlikely late night talk show host for CBS in 1989. His challenge to Johnny Carson's supremacy lasted just over a year.

I'd Like To Ask Myself Something

While hosting his own show, actor Keenan Ivory Wayans earned the dubious honor of being the only talk show host in history to interview *himself*. He was plugging his 1997 movie *Most Wanted*. Too bad it wasn't enough to save his own ratings!

Comedian Sinbad turned in a one-year-wonder stint as host of *Vibe* in 1997, a show which Sinbad took over from original host Chris Spencer only two months after the show's debut. But not even the talented comic could right the ship. *Vibe* went up against a show which starred *In Living Color* mastermind Keenan Ivory Wayans, which suffered the same short lifespan as Sinbad's show.

The Ugly
(And Unforgettable!)

You know who they are! These celebrities hosted talk shows that most viewers (and sometimes the hosts themselves!) would be very happy to forget, but somehow just can't seem to.

Canadian superstar Alan Thicke hosted an immensely popular daytime variety show in his native land. In 1983, Thicke introduced himself to American audiences for the first time with a late night talk show, *Thicke of the Night*. It was heavily advertised as a strong challenge to Carson, but Thicke couldn't live up to the incredible hype and his show was cancelled after one season. Although his talk show was universally recognized as a disaster, Thicke overcame it and has had a great television career on shows like *Growing Pains, Hope & Gloria* and the game show *Pictionary*.

APWWP

Chevy Chase, the talented *SNL* alum, was another disappointment as a talk show host.

Another entertainment legend who similarly fell on his face on the talk show circuit was a veteran of *Saturday Night Live,* Chevy Chase. With his comedic pedigree and popular movies like *Caddyshack* and *National Lampoon's Vacation* under his belt, the funny and popular Chase seemed like a good bet to host a show. But after only two months, Fox pulled the plug on the unqualified ratings disaster.

A more recent talk show debacle belongs to Los Angeles Lakers basketball legend Magic Johnson. Magic proved that it takes more than charisma and popularity to host a late-night talk show. *The Magic Hour* lasted an embarrassing eight weeks and never did find its footing. Detractors cited the lack of big-name

AP/WWP

Basketball star "Magic" Johnson could not find the magic formula for a successful talk show.

guests and Magic's obvious nervousness as reasons for the bad ratings. In fact, it took an appearance by shock jock Howard Stern, to boost his ratings to a respectable level!

In addition to these unforgettable underachievers, there's also a litany of hosts you could only put in the bizarre and unusual category. If there is a pioneer to the talk show sleaze format, it must be Morton Downey Jr. From 1988 to 1989, the chain smoking, right-wing attack dog (who now is a staunch anti-smoker, incidentally) not only played host to chaos on his show, but actively incited it whenever he could. You had to give him points for honesty – he didn't just trot out the spectacle and watch it happen, he got in there and rolled around with it!

Hot on the heels of Morton Downey Jr. was the bombastic Richard Bey, who added game show elements to the standard fiasco talk show format, such as mud wrestling for cash. Bey's show lasted until 1996 and Bey now claims he was pulled off the air for interviewing Clinton sex-scandal figure Gennifer Flowers. Of course, ratings probably had something to do with it!

Tough-talking, blustery Roseanne Barr moved from her sit-com hit *Roseanne* to a daily talk show in 1998 with horrific results.

Whoopi Goldberg finds herself in the clutches of
The Roseanne Show's host, Roseanne Barr.

The same person who screeched out the national anthem at a baseball game before grabbing herself and spitting on the ground gained only slightly more fans through her show, which technically lasted two seasons, although many station affiliates dropped it from their schedules after the first one.

Better known as Danny Partridge from the *Partridge Family* (and later famous for beating up a transvestite prostitute), Danny Bonaduce started a daytime talk show gig when he hosted *Danny!* in 1995. The show lasted only three months, but it helped Bonaduce launch a successful radio career, which carries on strongly today.

But Wait . . . There's More!
Don't forget these other talk show fly-by-nighters!

Bertrice Berry	Robin Givens	Mark Walberg
Tempestt Bledsoe	Marilu Henner	Marsha Warfield
Gordon Elliot	Vicki Lawrence	Rolanda Watts
Cristina Ferrare	Susan Powter	Chuck Woolery

The Box Office: How To Get Tickets For Your Favorite Show

Want to see your favorite show? Whether you want to hear or be heard, here are some ways to get yourself the best seats in the house.

If you are in Burbank, California:

The Late Late Show With Craig Kilborn
c/o On Camera Audiences
224 East Olive Avenue, #205
Burbank, CA 91502
cbs.com/latenight/latelate

The Tonight Show With Jay Leno
Tonight Show Tickets
3000 W. Alameda Avenue
Burbank, CA 91523
nbctv.nbci.com/tonightshow

If you are in Chicago:

The Jenny Jones Show
www.jennyjones.warnerbros.com or (312) 836-9485

The Jerry Springer Show
454 N. Columbus Drive, Second Floor
Chicago, IL 60611
(800) 96-JERRY or (312) 321-5365
www.jerryspringer.com

The Oprah Winfrey Show
www.oprah.com/tows/tows_landing.html or (312) 591-9222

If you are in Los Angeles:

Dennis Miller Live
www.hbo.com/dml/

The Dr. Laura Schlessenger Show
www.drlaura.com or (888) 730-4740

Politically Incorrect With Bill Maher
abc.go.com/primetime/politicallyincorrect/pi_home.html

If you are in New York:

The Charlie Rose Show
www.pbs.org/charlierose

Late Night With Conan O'Brien
NBC Tickets
30 Rockefeller Plaza
New York, NY 10112
nbctv.nbci.com/conan or (212) 664-3056/3057

The Late Show With David Letterman
cbs.com/latenight/lateshow

LIVE With Regis and Kelly
LIVE! Tickets
P.O. Box 777
Ansonia Station
New York, NY 10023-0777
tvplex.go.com/buenavista/livewithregis/index.html

Maury
www.studiosusa.com.maury

The Montel Williams Show
www.montelshow.com or (212) 989-8101

The Queen Latifah Show
Ticket Requests
PO Box 2656
G.P.O.
New York, NY 10199
latifahshow.warnerbros.com or (877) 485-7144

The Ricki Lake Show
www.rickishow.com

The Rosie O'Donnell Show
Tickets
30 Rockefeller Plaza
Suite 1400W
New York, NY 10112
rosieo.warnerbros.com

The Sally Show
www.sallyjr.com or (212) 244-3595

The View
Tickets "The View"
320 West 66th Street
New York, NY 10023
www.abc.go.com/theview/main.html

If you are in Washington D.C.:

Larry King Live
www.cnn.com/CNN/Programs/larry.king.live/index.html

Photo Index

Use this index to find photographs of individuals depicted in this book. Pages are listed in numerical order.

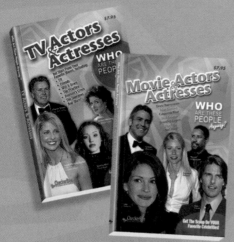